Praise for

Wrestling with Faith, Love, & Gators

"*Wrestling with Faith, Love, & Gators* is a winner! Whether you're young, old, or in between, you'll love Chad Young's style of writing. He mixes biblical truths while sharing his own life experiences. Some of which will make you shake your head and ask, 'what was he thinking?' Reading it is more like sitting around the dinner table swapping stories than reading a book. In fact, by the time you finish reading this book, you'll probably want to invite him to dinner!"

—**Lillian Duncan,** author of the Deadly Communications series

"Alligators, green biscuits, and lighting on a lake—the best part about Chad's masterful storytelling is that his illustrations really make the point clear and it sticks! My friend Chad is so real and authentic that his life perspectives in his book make you want to pursue Jesus and trust him enough to jump into an empty swimming pool, believing the Lord will fill it as you jump. His wisdom through Scripture and story makes you respond with, 'Well, of course! Why wouldn't I wholeheartedly surrender to Jesus?!'"

—**Roger Hershey,** Cru staff speaker, author of *The Finishers*

"Chad Young's *Wrestling with Faith, Love, & Gators* serves to remind us that the basic elements of being a disciple of Jesus Christ are found in the framework of the Great Commandment. Through personal stories, Scripture, and the words of an eclectic cadre of writers, Young provides insight and encouragement for young adults seeking to sort out the hard issues of life in the Light of Gospel Truth. Here is a book you will want to share with your Bible study group or with that skeptical friend who is seeking authentic answers to life's tough issues."

—**Rick Brewer,** PhD, president of Louisiana College

"*Wrestling with Faith, Love, & Gators* is a medley of scriptural anchors, modern day perplexities, inspirational testimonies, and Chad's self-deprecating anecdotes that all work together to serve as powerful, point-driving guidance. Each chapter helps make *Wrestling with Faith, Love, & Gators* both refreshing and eye opening, whether one is new to the faith or a long-time believer in need of renewal. Page after page, Chad writes with a steady mixture of maturity, wisdom, and humility, providing insightful answers to questions, old and new, about Christianity."

> —**Trent Fasnacht,** freelance home renovator/TV host —*American Rehab Charleston*, Blogger—*Blood, Sweat, and Pig's Ears*

"Through adventures with gators, spiders, waterbeds, and junior high bullies—and stories of real people, students, learning how to follow Jesus every day—Chad Young invites us into the astonishing adventure of loving God. Winsome, vivid, practical, insightful, sometimes hilarious, sometimes sobering, but always wise: this is a *good friend's* guide to what Jesus called the most important thing in life. Join the adventure!"

> —**Dr. David Horner,** professor of philosophy and biblical studies, Biola University, author of *Mind Your Faith: A Student's Guide to Thinking and Living Well* (IVP Academic)

"These days, it seems like everyone is talking about how to connect with millennials and younger generations in order to present Christian truth effectively. It is always a joy to come across a resource that does this well, and this is definitely the case with Chad Young's new book, *Wrestling with Faith, Love, & Gators*. In addition to having a really cool title, this book stirs the heart, informs the mind, and motivates the soul! Chad's ability to communicate truth via riveting stories and true-life accounts is what makes this book such a perfect work for the times in which we live. I highly recommend it."

> —**Alex McFarland,** director, Apologetics and Christian Worldview, North Greenville University, SC

WRESTLING
—WITH—
FAITH, LOVE,
& GATORS

WRESTLING —WITH— FAITH, LOVE, & GATORS

OVERCOMING BARRIERS TO FULLY LOVING GOD

CHAD YOUNG

LEAFWOOD
PUBLISHERS
an imprint of Abilene Christian University Press

WRESTLING WITH FAITH, LOVE, & GATORS
Overcoming Barriers to Fully Loving God

LEAFWOOD
P U B L I S H E R S
an imprint of Abilene Christian University Press

Copyright © 2016 by Chad Young

ISBN 978-0-89112-412-2

Printed in the United States of America

Published in association with the Blythe Daniel Agency, Inc., PO Box 64197, Colorado
Springs, CO 80962.

Cover design by Thinkpen Design, LLC
Interior text design by Sandy Armstrong, Strong Design

Leafwood Publishers is an imprint of Abilene Christian University Press
ACU Box 29138
Abilene, Texas 79699
1-877-816-4455
www.leafwoodpublishers.com

16 17 18 19 20 21 / 7 6 5 4 3 2 1

Dedicated to Dale and Bianca Freeman, my high school English teachers who taught me to write, believed in me, convinced me to take up drama after my football injuries, and who, still to this day, refer to me as "Charlie Brown."

Acknowledgments

I want to thank my beautiful wife, Elizabeth, my father, Herb Young, and my aunt, author Lillian Duncan, for their hard work helping me to edit this book. Without them, this project might not have been possible.

I also want to acknowledge Blythe Daniel of the Blythe Daniel Agency. She loves the Lord and lives out her faith in a way that impacts many.

There are so many others who have helped with editing and suggestions along the way, including my friends Rick James, Paul Gould, David Horner, Gabe O'Sullivan, Patrick Dickerson, Keith Bubalo, and Michael Anderson. There are too many to name all of them here.

Finally, I want to thank the college students and former students who shared their stories and made this book what it is today: Aaron Tripp, Eli Byrd, Erica Peterson, Sophia Array, Joy Pedrow, and Matt and Sabrina Pursley.

Table of Contents

Introduction

"Chad, jump on the gator's back!!"

Sixteen years ago I impulsively jumped on top of an alligator. Yes, you read that correctly. To most people in America, it's unusual even to see an alligator, but to Charlestonians in South Carolina, it's nearly an everyday event. In the Lowcountry area of that part of South Carolina, alligators have recently become an over-abundant nuisance; so much so that South Carolina created a hunting season to attempt to control their population.

During the six years my wife, Elizabeth, and I lived in Charleston, spotting alligators was as common as seeing blue jays in our neighborhood. We often shook our heads in disbelief at the neighborhood sign, "Slow . . . children at play," right above the "Beware of Alligators" sign. One alligator that inhabited a nearby pond nearly confronted Elizabeth one day while she was jogging and listening to her iPod. The alligator was crossing the street right then, and if a neighbor hadn't stopped Elizabeth by screaming and flagging her down, she likely would have encountered the gator head on.

My personal close encounter with an alligator occurred the day after my mother-in-law nearly lost her arm while weeding around their backyard pond. As she pulled weeds at the bank, unaware that an alligator lurked in the pond, the gator rose out of the water, snapping its jaws and barely missing her arm. This seven–and-a-half-foot alligator previously had been aggressive, and Elizabeth's parents had tried for a month to convince DNR (the Department of Natural Resources) to remove it before the incident. When Frank, Elizabeth's older brother, heard the alligator had nearly attacked his mother, he decided the time had come for the alligator to find a new home.

I'll never forget that day. I had arrived early at my future in-laws' house to pick up Elizabeth for a date. While waiting for Elizabeth, I followed Frank to the pond, curious to see how he planned to catch the alligator.

The wary reptile floated on the water's surface, watching us. Frank attached a chicken neck to a large hook on strong fishing line and cast it toward him. The gator quickly took the bait.

After the alligator swallowed the hook, Frank pulled the line while the gator thrashed, its huge tail slapping the surface of the pond. That day I witnessed the raw strength of the most powerful animal I'd ever seen.

Tugging the rope with all our might, Frank, another friend, and I pulled the gator up onto the bank. Without hesitation Frank jumped onto the alligator's back. Now I had always viewed Frank as being pretty fearless. He is an excellent hunter and fisherman and has played the star role in many near-death stories. From that point forward, however, my appreciation for his bravery rivaled my boyhood appreciation of Superman.

As Frank wrestled that huge, aggressive alligator, a strong fear knotted my gut, fear that things weren't going to turn out well. "Surreal" is the only word to describe the feeling that swept over me when the gator attempted the famous alligator "death roll" underneath Frank, who was grasping the alligator close to its head.

Trying to keep the alligator from rolling, Frank screamed, "Chad, jump on the gator's back!! Quick! I need help!"

For you to understand what happened next, it's important for you to know I'm a city boy who spent much of my childhood in Alabama. I had never been close to an alligator and was scared to death of this one that was doing the death roll in front of me. Another small detail was that I was dressed in the nicest clothes and shoes I owned, and this alligator was rolling in the mud.

Ultimately a subconscious devotion to Frank determined my decision of what to do. In that moment of fear, I cared about Frank, and I believed strongly that some things on this side of eternity are more important than dying. I probably didn't even understand how deeply I cared for Frank or how much I believed in eternity until the moment I decided to jump on top of that alligator.

I landed on the alligator's back, right above its hind legs and very close to the tail. It took all of my strength and Frank's to hold the alligator still and to keep it from doing the death roll. Finally, we were able to tie the alligator's legs behind its back and tape its jaws together with duct tape.

Frank didn't seem like he had thought about what to do with the alligator after we captured it. He was so determined to protect his parents from it that he hadn't planned ahead. While we dragged the alligator to a nearby tree to secure it, a neighbor spotted us and called the police. The police arrived and threatened to arrest Frank (it was illegal at that time to capture alligators), but after finding out that he had repeatedly contacted DNR for help, the police understood the dilemma my in-laws were in. DNR came and retrieved the gator, and we've enjoyed telling the story ever since.

Why did Frank capture the alligator? Why did I choose to jump on top of that monster and help Frank? Why did a neighbor call the police? Why did the police decide not to press charges against Frank?

It came down to this, which is true for all of us: we all had beliefs about life and love, about what is most important, and we all acted on those beliefs. Can you recall a time when you acted on some deep beliefs you had? No doubt you didn't care what it cost you, because you were determined to do what was needed.

Our spiritual lives are a lot like that too.

Over the years, I've had many ups and downs as a follower of Christ. At times I would do anything for Jesus (kind of like jumping on an alligator for Frank), and then at other times I got distracted, especially by the busyness of life, and didn't keep my priorities.

What would have happened to my relationship with Frank if I had been distracted while he was wrestling that alligator? Or if I had chosen not to get involved but simply to watch? Our relationship would have suffered, to say the least.

There have been times when I've put God first, but also countless times I've put my career, my family, or myself first. And every time I let myself get sidetracked, I soon realized I was not truly satisfied. The only thing that has ever satisfied me completely is having a close relationship with God.

The Bible contains many rules, but it's not exactly a book of rules. It's a book about God, who he is, and how we can know him. When it comes to knowing God, one simple "rule" takes preeminence over all the others.

Jesus himself communicated this rule when the Pharisees asked him what the greatest commandment was. Jesus said, "You shall love the Lord your God with all your heart and with all your soul and with all your mind" (Matt. 22:37).

If there's one rule we must follow to have a relationship with God, life should be easy, right?

If only!

I've found that it's not that easy, though. And to love God? Surely that's something we can all stick with, right?

In this book I will share my story about what I've learned as I've tried hard to follow the greatest commandment. It isn't a story about how simple it is to follow God, as some of my crazy stories will attest, but it shows how one thing can satisfy our hearts.

That one thing is experiencing God's love.

Will you follow me in the journey to love him?

Part 1

All Your Heart

[Jesus said,] "You shall love
the Lord your God
with all your heart
and with all your soul
and with all your mind."

—Matt. 22:37

CHAPTER
~1~

Somebody's Watching Us

"Elizabeth!" I whispered. "Wake up!"

Elizabeth sat awkwardly on the uncomfortable chair next to my hospital bed. She had been struggling to sleep.

"Elizabeth!" I continued to whisper frantically, this time a little louder.

"Whatcha need?" she responded as she roused from briefly nodding off. *You've got to be kidding me*, I'm sure she thought to herself. *Why is he awake? The nurse said he'd sleep for hours.*

My leg and knee surgery two days earlier had resulted in severe bone pain. To add to my discomfort, deep-vein blood clots developed in my leg, a dangerous side effect of the surgery. My right calf had swollen to the size of a small watermelon. Despite heavy doses of morphine, the excruciating pain had prevented me from sleeping at all during the past two days. I was severely sleep deprived.

"Elizabeth," I whispered forcefully, "we gotta get out of here! Somebody's watching us." I pointed to a box on top of the television with a red light on it. Convinced, I said, "Just look. There's a video camera on top of the TV. The spies are watching right now."

Knowing that I would not be in the mood for laughter, Elizabeth stifled a smile. Soothingly, she said, "No, honey, that's just the cable box for the television. That's not a camera."

"You're wrong!" I whispered as I looked at her seriously with wide eyes. "They call themselves doctors, but they are *not* doctors. They're trying to kill me and harvest my organs. We've got to get out of here right away!"

Her smile disappeared as she realized how seriously I believed what I was saying. *It's the medicine*, she thought to herself. The doctor, concerned over my lack of sleep, had prescribed a sleep aid, but he warned us that it could make me "goofy" or even cause hallucinations.

This was no laughing matter. Elizabeth realized that I was working my way to the edge of the bed to try to stand up and make my escape. I had clearly taken on the identity of a character from *The Conspiracy Theory*, *24*, or another of the many suspenseful action shows and movies I enjoy.

We'll return shortly to this true tale, which is also my kids' favorite bedtime story. They beg Elizabeth to retell it again and again, and to this day, they think the story of their daddy going crazy is the funniest thing they've ever heard.

To Elizabeth, however, that night was filled with fright. Who was this person so paranoid about spies? He didn't even sound like her husband. When would the medication wear off so that Chad could be Chad again? The irrational fear, *What if he'll always be like this?* crept into her mind, she told me later.

She couldn't wait for me to reclaim my identity and be the Chad she loved.

Elizabeth wanted the true Chad. But as I've heard her retell this story, I think sometimes I don't know who the real Chad is. As a believer in Christ, my thoughts often go awry when I don't spend time praying or studying my Bible daily. I forget that my identity is in Christ. My joy gets lost in my selfish thoughts and attitudes, or I forget I have a new life in Christ and become disobedient to God.

When we find our identities in other things besides Christ, such as our careers, athletics, friends, social networking, or even our sexual desires, we forget who we really are. Instead, we pursue fantasies and lifestyles the world offers that are the polar opposite of the Christian lifestyle God wants for us.

Whether we're plagued by guilt because of what we are doing or deliberately living in rebellion, we are distorting our true identity that's found in Christ.

In short, we all have an identity crisis.

Living our lives with the mistaken, borrowed, or distorted identity of the person we are without Christ isn't really living life at all. It causes terrible frustration, confusion, and danger to us and to those we love and share life with as well.

Identity Crisis

As Elizabeth was trying to calm my medicine-induced fears that night in the hospital room, I continued to whisper, "Distract the nurse while I get dressed. We're getting out of here!"

Her concern was growing.

Elizabeth knew I couldn't even walk to the bathroom, and another injury was inevitable if I tried to get out of bed. She rushed to the nurses' station to find our nurse. Allison had instructed Elizabeth to alert her if I became "too goofy."

As Elizabeth and Allison walked into my room, they discovered me sitting up in my hospital bed, pulling at my cables and tubes, attempting to get up.

Allison calmly said, "Hi, Mr. Young. Whatcha doing? Can I get you something?"

Looking guilty, I responded as if I was hiding something, "Oh, I don't need anything. I'm headed to the bathroom."

Allison was a professional, and she responded as if she was used to coaxing delusional patients into staying in bed. With a smile and a kindhearted tone, she said, "Oh, Mr. Young, maybe you don't have to go quite yet. You probably just have gas."

"What?" I spat in a passionate, defensive voice. "I've *never* had gas in my entire life!" I turned to Elizabeth with disgust and said, "How could you betray me like this? You! You are obviously one of them now."

Poor Elizabeth and Allison!

My hallucinations and shenanigans went on *all night long*, but somehow they managed to keep me in bed and keep me safe. I was convinced I had become a victim of a large plot to steal my organs. Elizabeth kept trying to tell me I was sleeping, and I kept saying, "Just look at my eyes! Do I look asleep?" The funny thing was that apparently I said this with my eyes closed. Elizabeth swears she will never let me take that sleep aid again.

Yes, I spewed ridiculous, hurtful comments during my period of being an overly paranoid, angry orthopedic patient. Fortunately, I can now blame my unkind words and actions on sleep deprivation and medication.

Often, though, when we find our identity in things besides Christ, we hurt ourselves and other people with our words, attitudes, and actions. And we can't or shouldn't make excuses for that.

In my experience in full-time ministry during this past decade, I've witnessed students claiming their identity in many good things besides Christ, such as being a straight-A student, an athlete, a video gamer, a boyfriend or girlfriend, the perfect son/daughter, a fraternity guy, a sorority girl, a student government leader, and so on.

One example of a student who struggled to find his identity in Christ is the former star quarterback for Charleston Southern University, Eli Byrd. This is what Eli had to say about his identity crisis:

> Finding your identity in anything other than Christ can leave you restless and empty. I say restless because any other identity is a false one. God made man in his image. Trying to make our image into something else is like telling a lie and then having to tell another to keep that one going, and then telling another lie to cover the previous lie, and the story continues. By the end of your busyness, you realize that your core being is still the same as it was before you allowed "the fake you" to allure others in. It is shameful to cover who you truly are because you want others to like you. Singer Lauryn Hill said it best: "The real you is more interesting than the fake you."
>
> That was me while I played football for Charleston Southern University. I was the quarterback, and there was a lot expected of me because of the position that I held. I tried my hardest to live up to all of the different expectations and denied who I truly was. I felt the tug of the Lord to abandon the praise of others and potential fortune to follow and serve him completely. Even though at the time it seemed to be a difficult decision and unwise in the eyes of some, I had to ask myself if I was going to serve the One who made me in his solid image no matter what, or put my trust in a faulty career.
>
> God doesn't call every athlete to give up his or her sport, but for me, the Lord made it clear after my junior

year that I needed to give up football in order to follow
him because it had become such an idol in my life. I
knew real joy could only come if I found my identity
in Christ. That point in my life was my greatest turning
point, and I can honestly say my life has been full of joy
and a real love for Christ ever since.

Personally, I know and understand Eli's struggle, because I've found
my identity in a lot of things besides Christ. In high school, I grew
to be an athlete and a good student. Not only did I dream of being
the top baseball player around, but I also desired all As in school.
There were times I found my identity in being the boyfriend of a
pretty girl, and I would go to great lengths to try to make everyone
believe I was a cool guy.

In college, I became the fraternity guy and a leader in student government. If I ever thought someone didn't like me or
find me worthy of their company, it bothered me to the core. I
wasted countless hours worrying about what people thought of
me. I would hide the real me and build the identity I thought they
wanted me to be. Then something happened that changed my life.

At the age of twenty, I began to have an authentic relationship
with God. A friend named James had strong faith, and he showed
me how to grow closer to Christ. I wish I could say I put God first
from that point on. However, college life was full of distractions,
and just because I prioritized my time with God one day didn't
mean I automatically put him first the next.

As I began to understand how badly I needed and desired God's
plan for my life, I became passionate about impacting others for
Christ and helping them to find authentic faith. I felt like I had
found the missing puzzle piece, and as I looked around, I saw so
many of my peers in college also searching and seeking wholeness.

It was then that I began to pour my heart and soul into ministering to others. I truly believed I was completely in God's will.

I didn't realize that I had begun a sinful habit that stuck with me for the next several years—putting ministry above my personal time with God.

We can get so busy doing good things for God that we can easily forget that he's a person, not a philanthropic project. God loves it when we do things for him *if* our hearts are in the right place—if we're taking time to know him and spend time seeking his direction. When our hearts aren't in the right place, God doesn't even consider our acts of service as worship toward him. "I appeal to you therefore, brothers, by the mercies of God, to present your bodies as a living sacrifice, holy and acceptable to God, which is your spiritual worship" (Rom. 12:1).

After I graduated from college, I got a job working as a process engineer in a paper mill. During the weekends and weekday evenings, I was active in church ministry as a Bible study leader, worship leader, youth leader, and children's ministry worker. One evening as I was spending time in prayer, confessing that I rarely spent time praying or studying the Bible, a thought popped into my head that I believe came from the Lord: *Chad, you can never do enough to earn my love. You're my child, and I simply love you.*

That's when I realized an important truth. If we give ministering to others a higher priority than our own personal relationship with God, then ministry can be just as sinful as stealing.

Since I began serving in full-time ministry fourteen years ago, I've had to constantly check my priorities by asking: *Why am I ministering?* I have to ensure it's due to a love of God and not due to a love of ministry.

Many people find their identities in ministry, family, sports, school, and careers. While these activities and people are of great value, they weren't meant to be the basis of our identity. In fact, if we place anything above God, including good things, the Bible says we are practicing a form of idolatry.

When God said, "You shall have no other gods before me" (Exod. 20:3), he wasn't just talking about worshipping statues and idols. He was saying that idolatry occurs when we begin to value anything more than we value God.

Jesus clarified this point in Luke 14.

As Jesus was making his way toward Jerusalem during the last part of his ministry, he turned to the crowd and said to them, "If anyone comes to me and does not hate his father and mother, his wife and children, his brothers and sisters—yes, even his own life—he cannot be my disciple" (Luke 14:26 NIV1984).

Now of course we know that Jesus didn't hate his family, nor does he want us to hate or neglect ours. Even while he was dying on the cross to save us from our sins, Jesus requested that his disciple John take care of his mother. Obediently, "this disciple took her into his home" (John 19:27 NIV1984).

In that speech to the crowd, Jesus was using hyperbole (obvious and intentional exaggeration) to make a point. He was simply saying that in comparison to our love for Christ, everything else should be a lower priority.

In the beginning, God created us to know him and have a relationship with him. By design, we were never meant to love anything or anyone more than we love him. When we place other people or things above God, trouble starts to mount in our lives. This trouble and frustration grows and grows like a giant balloon just waiting to pop.

Finding Our Identity in Christ

When I was fifteen, one of my friends broke a glass on my waterbed, and it was my responsibility to clean the mess. I drained the water out of the bed, vacuumed all the glass from around and underneath the water mattress, and then hooked up a garden hose from my bathroom sink to the mattress.

I watched for thirty minutes as the water started to fill up the mattress, but the process of filling the mattress was taking much longer than I ever expected. I decided to watch television downstairs while the mattress filled, and I still remember my father's words as I turned on the television. "Just be sure that you check the mattress every few minutes to make sure it doesn't fill up too much."

Well, there was a great episode of *Sanford and Sons* on television, and it didn't take long for me to get engrossed in the show. A little while later, I heard a loud thundering sound from up above. *Wow!* I thought to myself. *Was that lightning? It must have hit our house!*

"Chad, what was that?" my dad shouted. "Did you turn off the water?"

At that moment, my stomach sank and my heart skipped a beat. *Did that sound come from my room?* I sprinted up the steps and froze at the top, shocked by what I saw.

My waterbed resembled a giant, brown loaf of bread filling up my entire room. The "thunder" had been my bed frame bursting, and the water mattress was squeezing all of my belongings against the wall and crushing everything in sight. Thankfully, my father wasn't as stunned as I was. He darted past me and turned off the faucet.

As we inspected the bed, we discovered that the mattress was rock hard. If it had burst, it would have exploded like a bomb. I imagine it would have caused catastrophic damage to our house and probably washed me down the steps like a tidal wave.

I don't recall what my father said to me after that. Perhaps I've repressed his comments; the experience was so nearly calamitous. I do remember standing in the room for several hours, however, as all of the water drained into the bathtub. After we finally fixed the bed and put the appropriate amount of water back into the mattress, my water mattress was about the loosest in America.

Some nights I felt seasick as I tossed about on the waves rippling through that bed.

No, my bed would never be the same.

It had lost its firmness and had become irreversibly flexible.

The critical moment of my waterbed disaster occurred when I saw the condition of my waterbed. I stood there in disbelief, horrified at the sight of my mattress, knowing I was in huge trouble and that my bed was nearly destroyed.

Oddly, I didn't jump into action and turn off the water. It was like I was stuck, frozen, and not sure what to do first. If it hadn't been for my dad shutting off the water, the mattress easily could have burst, with devastating consequences to our house.

The sin in our lives can be like a swelling waterbed, weighing on us with devastating effects. As we continue to sin and put things ahead of Christ, we can do permanent damage to our lives emotionally, spiritually, and even physically.

Sometimes we believe the lie that it's too late and our sin is too great for God to forgive. We know we are in big trouble, but we think God gets tired of forgiving the same sin over and over again.

Perhaps sometimes other people, like our parents, step in to help us before our lives are destroyed, but often we don't listen to them when they try to help.

Some of us wait until too late to surrender our hearts completely to Christ. When we face a major crisis or fall into a sinful lifestyle, then we may turn to God, but our hearts and the hearts of those around us may get permanently damaged in the meantime.

Like my sad waterbed, we might never be the same if we continue to place other things in our lives as higher priorities than God. We may develop calloused and hardened hearts and become oblivious to our real identities that God created within us. Instead of agonizing over our shortfalls and past mistakes, we should rest in the fact that God gave us a new heart and a clean slate. "Therefore, if anyone is in Christ, he is a new creation. The old has passed away; behold, the new has come" (2 Cor. 5:17).

Jesus is waiting for us to come to him. "Come to me, all who labor and are heavy laden, and I will give you rest. Take my yoke upon you, and learn from me, for I am gentle and lowly in heart, and you will find rest for your souls. For my yoke is easy, and my burden is light" (Matt. 11:28–30).

It's our responsibility to find our identity in Christ. Only Jesus, the One who created us and knows our hearts better than we do, can give us the satisfaction we desire.

An important verse I've memorized to help me to remember my identity in Christ is Colossians 1:18: "He is the head of the body, the church. He is the beginning, the firstborn from the dead, that in everything he might be preeminent." Another translation uses the word "supreme" in place of "preeminent."

Jesus didn't die for us so that he could just be a passenger in our lives. He really didn't. He came and died for us so that he could be in the driver's seat with God as our co-pilot. When we received Christ as our Lord, we surrendered control of everything—our hopes, our dreams, our careers, our sexual desires, and yes, even our money.

By entering into God's family and becoming an adopted child of God, we agreed to let Christ be preeminent. When we fail to do that, we struggle to find the peace and joy God promises his children.

Without making Christ preeminent in our lives, we can't please God. We can only find our true identity and bear fruit of the best kind when our lives are in Christ.

With Christ, everything changes and we no longer find ourselves frustrated, spinning our wheels, trying to attain something that's out of our reach. When we find our identity in him, we find real happiness, an inner peace, and the satisfaction our hearts desire.

So how do we find our identity in Christ? Can we just say a prayer to God even if we've never prayed much before, and then things will totally change?

The answer is that an intimate relationship with Christ takes time, just as a relationship with a person takes time. We can't just flip a switch and make things better or reunite with the person we were intended to be with all along. We must invest the time necessary to know God and to develop a meaningful relationship with him, just as we would with someone we truly love.

In the following few chapters, we'll explore the reasons why knowing God is so critical to our spiritual well-being. The most important reason we should take the time to know God is that real joy can only be found in Christ. Let's take a look at how we can find our true and complete joy in him.

CHAPTER ~2~

Finding Real Joy

If you know anyone who has adopted a child, you are probably familiar with what a journey the process can be. Our adoption story began when Elizabeth and I were at a conference in Colorado five years ago. While casually visiting a ministry-fair booth, we learned about adoption through an adoption agency. At the time, our children were one, four, and seven, and honestly I felt like our home and hands were full. After hearing about the need for adoptive parents, however, I felt a stirring in my heart toward adoption. I just couldn't stop thinking about it.

On our way home from the conference, Elizabeth and I shared our equally growing desire to adopt. Knowing that adopting a child was a tremendous, life-changing decision, we didn't want to be hasty. We committed to pray about it for a year and to ask God if he wanted adoption for our family.

A year later, after much prayer and confirmation from the Bible, family, and friends, we concluded we were being called by God to adopt. Interestingly, both Elizabeth and I specifically felt led to adopt a biracial baby girl. We weren't sure why, but we kept saying, "I just think God is going to give us a mixed-race daughter."

Adopting is not for the fainthearted, as Elizabeth and I soon learned. The process was full of ups, downs, uncertainty, and hard decisions. I believe the most difficult step was filling out paperwork indicating what medical and behavioral problems we'd consider and checking off if we could handle mild, moderate, or extreme cases of each disability. There were a lot of tough decisions! Many of our friends wondered why we didn't just try for another pregnancy, and some seemed surprised when we told them we felt led to adopt a child of a different ethnicity.

During our home study, Beth,* the social worker who was in charge of our adoption, interviewed our kids. When she asked our son Wyatt, who was eight at the time, how he would feel if a child with a different skin color were placed in our home, he responded, "Oh, that would be no problem. I'd love her if she were blue, or red, or yellow, or even purple!"

Beth seemed to like his answer.

Actually, the interview with our children was quite nerve-racking. At least for us it was. Our oldest son is quite outspoken, and well, you just never know what he might say. For instance, he used to always say, "I can't wait until I can watch adult movies!" He meant PG or PG-13 movies, but obviously somebody could get the wrong idea. We talked with Wyatt about the importance of the interview and stressed that he needed to be honest.

We were scared to death that Wyatt would inadvertently say something to throw a monkey wrench into the adoption process. Beth interviewed both boys, and when she asked Wyatt what

---

*This name and future names in the book have been changed to protect people's privacy.

he liked to do for fun, Wyatt said, "Oh, I just like to play video games all the time, especially violent ones. You know, like the ones rated for everyone ten and up, even though I'm not ten yet." We about died. Now Wyatt only owned games for children under ten, and he had time limitations on how much he played. Sigh. Beth wrote furiously.

"What about reading, Wyatt? Do you like to read?"

Wyatt responded, "Oh, yes! I love to read. I just read a great book today called, *Gregor and the Curse of the Warmbloods*. It was great!"

Beth's eyes widened.

Again Beth wrote frantically, and our adoption hopes took another hit. I looked at Elizabeth with a questioning look; she just shrugged and shook her head. Fortunately, Beth then asked Wyatt to describe his personality, and he said, "Very shy." Beth immediately looked relieved as we think she realized that Wyatt might not be the most credible interviewee.

Eventually, despite the awkward interview moments, we were approved, but the rules would not allow us to indicate in our state adoption file that we wanted to adopt a biracial child. We could either say we wanted to adopt a child with our same ethnic background or that we were open to adopting a child of any race. For months, we waited for a phone call, wondering if we would be asked to adopt a Caucasian, African American, or Latino child, or one with another racial background.

One day, a pastor named John called from North Carolina, saying he had heard we were hoping to adopt. He said a young girl in his church had just delivered a baby, and her family was praying that a strong Christian family would adopt the baby girl.

John said, "There is one thing I want to share that might be a deal breaker for you."

"What is it?" I responded, made a little nervous by his tone.

"Well," John said, "The baby is biracial. The birth mother is Caucasian, and the birth father is African American."

I about dropped the phone. For months, Elizabeth and I had felt like the Lord placed a mixed-race child on our hearts during our prayers. "That's no problem at all," I shared. "In fact, I believe this is the baby girl we're supposed to raise."

A few long months later, we brought Josilynn home and have had the privilege of calling her our daughter. A number of times people have commented that Josilynn is fortunate to have three siblings who love her so dearly, but Elizabeth and I have always felt that we're the fortunate ones.

Elizabeth once asked if I thought Josilynn had inherited my sinus problems. I replied, "Honey, I think that would be impossible." We had a good laugh over how easy it is to forget that she can't inherit our medical problems.

Yes, she's truly a member of the Young family!

One of the most amazing things about God is that when we place our faith in his Son, Jesus, he literally adopts us into his family. One of my favorite passages is Ephesians 1:4–6: "For he chose us in him before the creation of the world to be holy and blameless in his sight. In love, he predestined us to be adopted as his sons through Jesus Christ, in accordance with his pleasure and will—to the praise of his glorious grace, which he has freely given us in the One he loves" (NIV 1984).

Through Josilynn, I've learned more about the grace of God. As soon as we are adopted, he loves us unconditionally, whether we're good or bad. In fact, on this side of heaven we're never completely good. We'll always have a sinful nature until the day we go to be with God forever.

When Josilynn does something bad and gets in trouble, I find myself afterward telling her, "I want you to know that I love you, no matter what. I love you when you're good. I love you when you're bad. I just plain and simply love you."

God is just like that, even more than that, since he is the perfect Father.

Being Loved Versus Experiencing Love

Now there's an important difference in being loved unconditionally and experiencing that love. When Josilynn hits her sister, Evelyn, in the head with a plastic baseball bat on purpose, she doesn't experience my love, at least temporarily. She experiences my anger and discipline.

God is the same way with us.

He always loves his adopted children, but when we try to find joy in other things besides Christ, he has to discipline us. He loves us too much to let us think that anything else besides Christ can give us the deep joy our hearts really crave.

We've all tried to find joy in other places apart from God. Working with college students, I've seen young people seek to find joy in relationships, sex, drugs, playing video games, and even doing ministry. One of the most common places I've found students trying to find joy is in winning the approval of others.

To be quite honest, I've always been obsessed with making people like me.

Back in the third grade, my teacher asked the class to think about what they wanted to be when they grew up. Trying to get a laugh, I proclaimed that I hoped to own my own junkyard like Fred Sanford in a popular television show, *Sanford and Sons*.

But when those laughs didn't appease my obsession with making my friends laugh, I did the unthinkable when it was time for Angie Felton, the cutest girl in my class, to share.

Every boy in our class, including me, had a crush on Angie. When she told the class she wanted to be a lawyer when she grew up, I was as shocked as everyone else when I interjected, "You mean you want to be an underwear saleswoman!"

For nine-year-old boys, the word "underwear" is a hilarious word. When I suggested Angie Felton desired to be an underwear saleswoman, I'm confident the roar from my classroom was heard by everyone in the entire school building. I'll never forget the look of horror in Angie Felton's eyes at that moment.

Poor Angie. Despite my crush on her, I completely disregarded her feelings in order to make others laugh and like me. It didn't matter who I hurt. I would do anything to seek joy in the approval of others. It was an obsession, really.

I'll never forget what my third-grade teacher said to me after class that day when I apologized to her for disrupting the class. She said, "Chad, you don't need to apologize to me. You need to apologize to Angie. You might not have seen it, but while you and your friends were laughing your heads off at your underwear joke, Angie started crying. She didn't make a scene of it, but she got up from her seat, excused herself, and went to the bathroom so she could cry by herself. Chad, you didn't just disrupt my class. That's the least of what you did. I'm upset with you because you broke Angie Felton's heart."

I felt obsessed with finding joy in others' acceptance, and I'm ashamed now at how I'd do anything to earn it . . . even if it meant hurting others.

You may be like this too. You worry about what people think of you. While you may not be concerned about what *everyone* thinks of you, you are concerned about what *someone* thinks of you, and you're committed to seeking his or her approval. We've all bought into the lie that joy comes from what others think of us.

Let's look at the story of the two sons in Luke 15:11–32 and see what Jesus has to say about the ultimate source of joy and how to find it in him.

The Lost Sons

Before we can understand the story of the two sons, it's important to look at Luke 15:1–3 so we know who Jesus is telling the parable to:

"Now the tax collectors and sinners were all drawing near to hear him. And the Pharisees and the scribes grumbled, saying, 'This man receives sinners and eats with them.' So he told them this parable."

While Jesus was talking to the tax collectors and sinners, he was primarily addressing the Pharisees, who were looking down their noses at the tax collectors and "sinners" while questioning who Jesus was if he would allow such disgusting people to hang out with him.

One thing we know about the Pharisees when we read about them in the Bible is that they didn't love Jesus. The Pharisees represent us when we don't follow the Great Commandment to love God. We are Pharisees when we get caught up in being a good person or just doing Christian activities instead of simply being in love with Jesus.

When we study the Pharisees, we also learn that they cared very much about what people thought of them. On the outside, they followed the laws from the Old Testament, but they did it so they would look good, not because they loved God. Basically, when we worry about what others think of us, we are much like the Pharisees.

Now let's look at the parable of the lost sons in Luke 15:11–24. While it's a bit lengthy, it's one of the clearest parables in the Bible showing exactly how we can either experience real joy in Christ or how we can miss it. It shows not only what it looks like when we're not in love with God but also how we can receive his love:

> And he said, "There was a man who had two sons. And the younger of them said to his father, 'Father, give me the share of property that is coming to me.' And he divided his property between them. Not many days later,

the younger son gathered all he had and took a journey into a far country, and there he squandered his property in reckless living. And when he had spent everything, a severe famine arose in that country, and he began to be in need. So he went and hired himself out to one of the citizens of that country, who sent him into his fields to feed pigs. And he was longing to be fed with the pods that the pigs ate, and no one gave him anything.

"But when he came to himself, he said, 'How many of my father's hired servants have more than enough bread, but I perish here with hunger! I will arise and go to my father, and I will say to him, "Father, I have sinned against heaven and before you. I am no longer worthy to be called your son. Treat me as one of your hired servants."' And he arose and came to his father. But while he was still a long way off, his father saw him and felt compassion, and ran and embraced him and kissed him. And the son said to him, 'Father, I have sinned against heaven and before you. I am no longer worthy to be called your son.' But the father said to his servants, 'Bring quickly the best robe, and put it on him, and put a ring on his hand, and shoes on his feet. And bring the fattened calf and kill it, and let us eat and celebrate. For this my son was dead, and is alive again; he was lost, and is found.' And they began to celebrate.

"Now his older son was in the field, and as he came and drew near to the house, he heard music and dancing. And he called one of the servants and asked what these things meant. And he said to him, 'Your brother has come, and your father has killed the fattened calf, because he has received him back safe and sound.' But he was angry and refused to go in. His father came out and entreated him, but he answered his father, 'Look, these many years I have served you, and I never disobeyed your command, yet you never gave me a young goat, that I might celebrate with my friends. But when this son of yours came, who has devoured your property with prostitutes, you kill the fattened calf for him!' And he said to him, 'Son, you are always with me, and all that is mine is yours. It was fitting to celebrate and be glad, for this your brother was dead, and is alive; he was lost, and is found.'"

Notice the lavish love of the father. He didn't just welcome the younger son home. He ran out to meet him. Since it wasn't socially appropriate for a wealthy, older man in Jewish society to run,[1] this demonstrates that the father was so happy to see his son that he set aside all social norms to run and greet him.

The father then dressed the younger son in the finest clothing. He put a ring on his finger, a symbol to everyone that the son had been reconciled to the family.

And the fattened calf was killed for a joyful celebration. In Jewish culture, a fattened calf was saved for very special occasions. Killing this calf signified that the father was full of joy and the younger son was to experience that joy with his father.

In the meantime, the older son was coming in from the fields from a hard day's work. Remember, he had stayed home to work hard and be a good son. As he was approaching his father's house, he heard what sounded like singing and dancing. What in the world was going on?

He asked someone what was happening, only to discover that his father was throwing a welcome-home party for his despicable brother. Angry, the older brother refused to join the party, even after the father came out to meet him in a similar way as when he ran out to meet the younger son.

Three Truths from the Story of the Lost Sons

There are three truths in this passage that we should apply to our lives. First, we can never stray so far away from God that he won't run out to meet us when we come back to him. The younger son squandered his father's wealth, worked for a Gentile (a no-no in Jewish culture), and labored as a pig herder (pigs were considered filthy in Jewish culture). And yet the father still poured out his lavish love on this son when he returned.

Let me share the story of a Charleston Southern University student, Tamara (not her real name). Her story demonstrates that we can never stray so far away from God that he won't pour out his incredible love when we come home to him. Tamara, a single mother of a two-year-old, was living with her boyfriend off campus. One of the student leaders involved in our ministry at CSU, Melissa, was talking to Tamara after class one day, sharing the message of Christianity.

Tamara said, "I know I need Christ in my life, but I have to get my life straight first. Then I can get things right with God."

Melissa thought for a moment and asked, "If your daughter fell down and scraped her knee, would you want her to bandage her leg first and then come to you for comfort and help, or would you want her to come to you first so the two of you could fix her hurts together?"

Tamara said, "That's easy. Of course, I'd want her to come to me first."

"It's the same with God," Melissa replied. "He doesn't want us to get our lives together first and then come to him. We can never get our lives straight without him. He wants us to come to him and let him mend our broken lives."

We know Melissa's statement to Tamara is true. God does want us to come to him first so he can mend our brokenness. We're not supposed to "get our lives straight" before we approach him. We can never stray so far away that he won't accept us in our brokenness. That day Tamara experienced God's undiluted love when she reached out to God in her brokenness and asked Jesus to be her Lord and Savior. Just as the father in the parable embraced his youngest son, God embraced Tamara.

The second thing we learn from this parable is that we can never experience God's love if we seek joy in what we do or what others think of us. The younger son would have continued to live an empty life if he had not humbled himself and returned to his father. The older son, representing the Pharisees, was proud of himself for being the "good son." He was probably concerned with what others thought of him or the blessings he thought he deserved. The father came out to meet him, but he missed out on experiencing his father's love by refusing to come to the party. It's kind of like I explained earlier with my daughter Josilynn—there's a difference in being loved unconditionally and experiencing that love. While the older son was loved by his father, he didn't experience it.

After I began a more meaningful relationship with God in my college days, I was much like the older son in the parable. I desired to look good on the outside so that others would think I was more spiritually mature. I even led a Bible study in my fraternity, but most of the guys probably saw right through my pious activities. I still wasn't experiencing joy in Christ on a daily basis. Yes, there were times when I was joyful, especially when I attended church or ministry functions, but I wasn't experiencing it on a daily, moment-by-moment basis.

This brings us to the third lesson from the story: we must connect with Jesus every day and see the depth of our sin so we can experience the height of God's love and live a joyful, mountaintop life. Jesus used the parable to explain to the Pharisees why the "sinners" were drawing near to him but the Pharisees were not. They were missing out on the heights of true joy because they failed to see the depth of their sin.

We're all in danger of missing out on the complete joy as well . . . if we miss out on seeing the depth of our sin and our need for a Savior. God pours out his lavish love on those who are broken and recognize the depth of their sin.

I love how the story with the older son ends. After telling the older son that his blessings were there all along for that son to enjoy, the father left it up to him. He didn't flog the older son for refusing to come to the party. He simply told him, "I'm here, ready to fellowship with you when you come to me. And when you come to me, I'll pour out my love on you too."

This makes me want to come to Jesus, confess my sins of self-righteousness, and experience his limitless love. That's where overwhelming joy is found. It's found in our brokenness before the Lord.

Earlier I told you our adoption story. Soon after we brought Josilynn home, Elizabeth was out grocery shopping with our four kids and her niece who was visiting for the day.

As Elizabeth checked out, the cashier was listening to all the children asking Elizabeth for treats and candy at the register. The cashier commented, "You have your hands full. These children aren't all yours, are they?"

"No," replied Elizabeth. "Only four of the five are mine."

The cashier scoffed and responded, "Well, I figured that much!"

Elizabeth bit her tongue and thought to herself, *Hmmm . . . you figured that much? Well, you figured wrong.* But then she brushed it off without saying anything.

Clark, our son who was six years old at the time, never misses a beat. As Elizabeth was pushing the shopping cart through the parking lot, he asked, "Mom, did you hear that lady ask if all of us were your kids back there? You know you should have explained which ones of us are your kids. Because, you know Wyatt? Well, he doesn't really look like the rest of us. She probably thought he didn't belong in our family."

Elizabeth just smiled and said, "You're right, Clark. Next time I will be sure to point out that Wyatt does belong in our family."

It clearly never occurred to Clark that Josilynn's skin tone would set her apart in some eyes. To Clark, Josilynn isn't an adopted family member. She is his beloved sister.

In the same way, God simply treasures us once we enter into his family. He has children from different ethnicities all over the world. One day, people from every tribe and tongue will worship him in heaven. Together, we'll experience the boundless love of the Father for all eternity.

Note

[1]Taken from Wayne Grudem's and Thomas Schreiner's study notes in the *ESV Study Bible* (Wheaton: Crossway, 2008), 1989.

CHAPTER ~3~

The Pearl of Great Value

The summer before eighth grade, my family moved from Cullman, Alabama, to Valley, Alabama, when my dad took a new job pastoring a church. Wow, that was a tough move for me. No doubt you remember how tough junior high school can be for any teenager. Most have their own horror stories to tell from that time in life. I would never want to relive those junior high years again.

Like most insecure thirteen-year-olds, I was desperate to fit in at my new school. I walked into my physical education class my very first day thinking, "Oh, please, please like me, people!"

I was standing on a baseball field as PE began when an older guy named Jimmy walked up. Jimmy sported a mullet haircut, wore stone-washed jeans, and had the thickest brown mustache of anyone at Valley Junior High (or Valley High, for that matter!).

I figured that he must have been at least sixteen. He was a man among thirteen-year-old boys in my eighth-grade PE class.

Looking back, when I think about middle school and boys, there seemed to be three categories: ones who had not hit puberty yet, those who had, and those who had failed multiple grades and were basically men. Yep, the last group included the ones with mustaches, and those in the first two groups knew to steer clear of them.

As Jimmy approached, I thought to myself, *Whoa, that's one big mustache. I hope this guy doesn't kill me.*

I was pleasantly surprised when Jimmy stopped in front of me, flashed me a friendly smile, and offered his hand for me to shake. With a big grin, he said, "My name's Jimmy. What's yours?"

"Oh," I responded with relief. "My name's Chad. Nice to meet you, Jimmy." I then stuck out my hand to shake his.

But before I could shake his hand, Jimmy reached up with his other hand, grabbed mine with a firm grip, and shouted, "Welcome to Valley Junior High, son!" He then pulled out a razor blade and swiped it across my arm.

I looked down in horror as blood started squirting from my arm! *What the heck?* I thought. *Is this really happening to me?*

It did happen. My arm had to be stitched, and my parents met with the principal the next day to demand that Jimmy be expelled from school. The principal, who was a member of my dad's church, said, "We see this happen every year. These kids who are about to turn sixteen can't legally drop out of school. So they stick around until their sixteenth birthday and then drop out. Jimmy will be sixteen in a couple of months, and I'm expecting him to drop out like the others."

My parents and I were horrified. After a three-day suspension, Jimmy returned to school, rejoined the other guys with mustaches, and continued terrorizing those of us without mustaches for the remainder of the school year.

A week after the cutting incident, I was humiliated and humbled again at basketball tryouts. Expecting to be a star player like I had been in the parks-and-recreation league in Cullman, I was one of only two Caucasian kids who tried out for the team. When I made the cut, one of the African American guys who didn't make the team told me, "You just made the team because they had to have white boys. It's reverse discrimination." In hindsight, he may have been correct. I rode the bench the entire season. Two of my teammates could dunk the ball, and I wasn't even tall enough to touch the net when I jumped. I felt desperate to fit in and lived in misery those first few months in Valley when I didn't.

What I'd forgotten at the time was that a few months prior to moving to Valley, I had become a follower of Christ by asking Jesus to come into my life. For a short time that summer, I became passionate about Jesus. After we moved, however, my desire to fit in and have friends took first place in my life. I'd inadvertently pushed Jesus to the back of my mind so I could focus on my new priorities.

As I look back on this time, I realize how grieved God must have been when I set my relationship with him aside to pursue fitting in with others. I never meant to put anything ahead of God. Yet many times in my teen years and even my adult life I've done just that. At other times I've turned my back on God completely by living a sinful lifestyle.

Whether you realize it or not, you're probably like this too. Maybe you've turned your back on God by treasuring other things besides Christ. Maybe you've searched for joy and happiness in all the wrong places. Maybe you're like so many others who have bought into the lie that joy comes from earthly treasures and not from the overflowing love of Jesus.

In the previous chapter, we talked about how we can receive God's love or, rather, how it is that we enter into the kingdom of heaven. When we run to the Father as the prodigal son did, we can experience real joy. In this chapter, let's examine what should be true of us once we become Christians.

Let's look at two short parables in Matthew 13 and see what Jesus has to say about the kingdom of heaven. In order to understand these parables, we need to know that one of the themes of the book of Matthew is that Jesus is the King that God promised throughout the Old Testament. Matthew even opens his Gospel with the lineage of Jesus, showing that Jesus is a direct descendant of King David. When David became king of Israel, he received a promise from God that one of his offspring would be the king of a kingdom that would have no end.

God's kingdom is the greatest treasure the world has ever known, and if we store up treasures in heaven, God will give us the joy our hearts desire. However, as Matthew states in 6:19–21, if we store up for ourselves earthly treasures, we are seeking to find joy in temporary things that will fade away.

In Matthew 13, we find Jesus' shortest two parables: "The kingdom of heaven is like treasure hidden in a field, which a man found and covered up. Then in his joy he goes and sells all that he has and buys the field. Again, the kingdom of heaven is like a merchant in search of fine pearls, who, on finding one pearl of great value, went and sold all that he had and bought it" (13:44–46).

Picture a man discovering a treasure buried in a field. In first century Israel, they didn't have banks. They didn't have a stock market or mutual funds. When someone wanted to set aside money for retirement, they simply went out into a field and buried it, like a squirrel buries a nut and expects to dig it back up at a later date.

Realizing the great value of the treasure he found, the man in the parable went out and sold all of his possessions in order to purchase the land and possess the treasure. In this brief parable Jesus is telling us that he wants to be the greatest treasure in our lives, more valuable than all of our possessions combined. That's a pretty bold statement from a very bold man, isn't it? Its boldness may explain in part why the Pharisees wanted to have him put to death. Does it sound arrogant to you? Well, it isn't arrogant if God is the only one who can truly bring satisfaction and wholeness to our lives.

The second parable in the same passage above is about a pearl merchant. Considering that this parable is only two verses, it says a lot about who we are and what we should do when we enter the kingdom of God by making Christ the King of our lives.

The Parable of the Pearl of Great Value

Picture a pearl merchant who owns many pearls and has spent his whole life buying and selling pearls. He's seen every kind of pearl the world has to offer. He's seen beautiful pearls. He's seen large pearls, expensive pearls, rare pearls, odd-looking pearls, and cute little pearls. He's seen them all and owned many of them at one time or other.

However, one day this pearl merchant finds a pearl that is so valuable it is beyond everything he has ever seen or owned put together. No matter the cost, he has to have the pearl. So he goes out and sells every pearl he has in his valuable collection so that he can purchase the one pearl that puts all others to shame.

There are a few principles from this passage that we should apply to our lives. First, we all have "pearls" in our lives that cause us to turn away from Christ. Tim Keller has a helpful way of explaining this. In some of his sermons on Jesus' parables, he refers to two tests he calls the solitude test and the nightmare test.[1]

The solitude test is this: Where does your mind go in solitude? When the busyness of life is hushed, what do you think about? What are your fantasies? Financial security? A relationship or the dream of a relationship? Whatever your mind drifts toward during times of solitude, those things are your heart's treasure.

The nightmare test is similar: What are your worries? What are your fears? Losing someone or something? Getting accepted by people who matter? Whatever you fear losing the most reveals what you love the most.

When I'm in solitude, one of the things my mind can drift toward is financial security. Have I saved enough for retirement? If I pass away, will my wife, Elizabeth, and our kids be taken care of financially? You may not struggle with this now, but you probably will as you begin to plan for your future.

Some of your pearls now may include sexual gratification, your career, what major to pursue in school, getting all As, or your boyfriend or girlfriend. Perhaps your worries consume your thoughts. Whatever you treasure the most, whatever your mind drifts toward in solitude, these are the pearls in your life.

Another principle from the pearl merchant parable is that counterfeit pearls will never satisfy us completely the way that God can. Think about the story for a minute. The pearl merchant already had a lot of "stuff," but he still didn't have enough. There was still a pearl, representing Christ in this parable, which was more valuable than everything he owned combined.

Winning in college football is a good example of how our culture can never get enough of something. Being a graduate of Clemson University, I love college football, and for many years it wasn't pretty for us Clemson fans. Over and over the football team let its fans down. Several years ago, ESPN commentators even coined a term, "pulling a Clemson." They used it to describe teams that lost to teams they should have beaten.

In 2012 and 2013, however, the Tigers actually had two of the best seasons in Clemson history. For the first time, they won eleven games in back-to-back years. They beat the LSU Tigers in a bowl game to end one season, and then they beat the Ohio State Buckeyes in the Orange Bowl the next year.

And how did many Clemson fans feel after the season? Shouldn't all Tigers fans have been happy to have the two most exciting teams in decades? No, many were disgusted that we lost to our state rival, the South Carolina Gamecocks, both years. Some felt that their football team still had let them down.

College football is just one light-hearted example, but I can think of many more serious ones. Young adults often pursue destructive counterfeit pearls such as promiscuous relationships, consuming too much alcohol, or experimenting with drugs. Some counterfeit pearls such as making lots of money or being a video "gamer" may not seem destructive on the surface, but they can put our relationship with Jesus on the back burner. This can lead to a lack of passion and love for the Lord. Therefore they can be destructive to our spiritual lives.

A counterfeit pearl can never bring complete satisfaction because you can never have enough of it, and it has a false value.

A third principle from this passage, and probably the most important, is that belonging to Jesus costs us something. In the parable, the pearl merchant had to sell all he had in order to purchase the pearl of great value. By including this in the parable, Jesus emphasized that following him requires a great sacrifice.

King David understood that true worship costs the worshipper. At the end of 2 Samuel, disease was spreading because the king violated God's restrictions on census taking. David bought a threshing floor in order to build an altar there to worship God and further avert the plague. The man who owned it tried to give David the threshing floor as well as oxen and wood for burnt offerings. The king's wise response was, "No, but I will buy it from you for a price. I will not offer burnt offerings to the LORD my God that cost me nothing" (24:24).

The Apostle Paul also understood that worship comes at great cost. In Romans 12:1 he said: "I appeal to you, therefore, brothers, by the mercies of God, to present your bodies as a living sacrifice, holy and acceptable to God, which is your spiritual worship."

Right now, there are Christians sitting in prisons around the world, and their only crime is that they worship Jesus. According to the World Watch List research group, more than two thousand Christians have been martyred for their faith in the country of Nigeria alone in the past seventeen months.[2] These Christians understand that loyalty to Jesus costs.

When we surrender our lives to God, he brings us into his eternal spiritual kingdom where Christ is King. Our new spiritual reality is that we can no longer be kings of our own lives. We can no longer just do whatever we want to do. Our lives belong to Jesus, and if we allow him to do in us what he wants to do, the life he has in store for us will be so much better than we could imagine.

I love George MacDonald's parable that C. S. Lewis paraphrased in *Mere Christianity*:

> Imagine yourself as a living house. God comes in to rebuild that house. At first, perhaps, you can understand what He is doing. He is getting the drains right and stopping the leaks in the roof and so on; you knew that those jobs needed doing and so you are not surprised. But presently He starts knocking the house about in a way that hurts abominably and does not seem to make sense. What on earth is He up to? The explanation is that He is building quite a different house from the one you thought of—throwing out a new wing here, putting on an extra floor there, running up towers, making courtyards. You thought you were being made into a decent little cottage: but He is building a palace. He intends to come and live in it Himself.[3]

In what ways is God knocking on your house in a way that hurts? What areas of your house does God want to work on next? If your worship doesn't seem to be costing you anything, it may be time to ask God if he wants you to give up or sacrifice something that is a counterfeit pearl.

Our worship comes at a cost, but God promises that the payoff is more incredible and more valuable than we ever thought possible. We thought he was just building a cottage, but he's building a mansion!

Joy Pedrow's Story

God has so much in store for us, and my friend Joy Pedrow's life is a great example of this. Joy is a rising senior at the University of South Florida in Tampa, and her story is common in what I'm seeing today on college campuses. Joy is passionate for the Lord. Really, that's an understatement. She wasn't always so passionate about God, though. Once, she was more passionate about a young man she fell in love with, and that was keeping her from loving God with all her heart. I asked Joy to share her story, and these are her words:

> In high school, I was dating a guy who was also one of my best friends. The problem was that I believed he completed me, and thus my biggest fear was losing him. I made him "my everything." He was all I thought about and talked about. I could not picture life without him. Recently, I reread my high school journal and found an entry about him. I wrote, "I'm scared to lose him. Fear is plaguing my thoughts. I can't picture my life without him. He is my best friend. I tell him everything. If we break up or if something happens to him, I would be heartbroken."
>
> I had made him a counterfeit pearl without even knowing it.

By making him my everything, I couldn't picture my life without him. In high school, relationships are a big deal. Culture and media tell girls that a boyfriend will complete her by making her feel loved and beautiful, just like a princess. We don't understand the big picture. We have our whole life to live, God willing, and this one relationship will look small in a couple years. But in that moment he was my life.

Our relationship lacked boundaries—physical, emotional, and spiritual. Because of this lack of boundaries, the breakup left me crushed. When a person becomes "your everything" and then they are gone, the pain is overwhelming. When we broke up, I realized that his "love" was not satisfying. I had made my boyfriend my counterfeit pearl because, at the time, I did not understand that only God's love could complete me. This pearl left me in a constant state of fear, unlike Jesus, who gave me peace.

Like Joy, we need to give God first place in our lives. When we do, he will do greater things in and through us than we can ever imagine. This past year Joy started a ministry called "Joy Pedrow Ministries" in which she mentors young women and helps them to grow in their faith. She's absolutely passionate about helping girls give Christ first place in their lives.

Had Joy not walked away from her counterfeit pearls to follow Christ, she would have never started this ministry.

After reading Joy's story, you may be thinking, "I probably am valuing many things above Christ. How do I just get rid of my counterfeit pearls?"

The answer is simple. We must know and understand the value of Jesus, our one great pearl. We can do this by taking the time to connect with Jesus every day through prayer, reading the Bible, and meditating on him. All who fail to walk daily with Jesus are in danger of missing out on the depth of the joy we experience when Jesus is our first love.

Some of your counterfeit pearls may fit into the "destructive and dangerous" category mentioned above, but some of your counterfeit pearls may be good things, such as a relationship or a hobby.

Before you start cutting off relationships or hobbies to rid yourself of counterfeit pearls, spend time with God. Ask him to reveal what, if anything, is preventing you from putting God first. If something needs to go, God will reveal this to you when you ask him for wisdom. The important thing is that we need to give God first place.

Here's what we learn from Jesus' parable of the Hidden Treasure and the parable of the Pearl of Great Value: God pours out great joy on those who understand the value of Christ and surrender their counterfeit pearls for him.

I love how the book of Matthew ends.

After Jesus gave his Great Commission to his disciples, the very last thing he said to them was: "Behold, I am with you always, to the end of the age" (28:20). It's as if he was saying, "I'm not just a temporary treasure like your counterfeit pearls. My joy is an eternal joy, and if you follow me, you will be satisfied forevermore."

This makes me want to return to Jesus, confess my sin of coveting counterfeit pearls, and experience his unlimited love again. That's where overwhelming joy and real treasure are found—only in an authentic relationship with Jesus.

Earlier I told you the story of my struggles to fit in with the crowd during my junior high years. Do you know how many times recently I've been upset that I didn't fit in my first few months at Valley Junior High? Zero times.

I struggled socially and emotionally for a few months, but eventually I developed a group of friends and forgot all about the tough months. That's the way it is with counterfeit pearls. We think they're so special and wonderful, and we may even think we need them. However, they are only temporary and can never satisfy our hearts forever.

We all have the chance right now to experience the joy of having the pearl of great value, the treasure that satisfies our hearts eternally. Will you walk away from your counterfeit pearls and return to Christ? It will be easier once we understand the value of Christ. In the next chapter, we'll explore ways that we can better understand just how valuable he is.

Notes

[1] Tim Keller's sermons on Jesus' parables, including the parable of the pearl of great value, can be downloaded free, thanks to a generous donation, on Redeemer Presbyterian Church's website, http://sermons2.redeemer.com/sermons/parable-pearl-priorities.

[2] Jerry Dykstra, *Nigeria Tops Christian Persecution Violence List: New Open Doors Report.* (June 2013): Accessed January 16, 2015, https://www.opendoorsusa.org/newsroom/tag-news-post/nigeria-tops-christian-persecution-violence-list/.

[3] C. S. Lewis, *Mere Christianity* (New York: HarperCollins, 2009), Kindle edition, book 4, chap. 9.

Attack of the Caterpillar

Eleven years ago, my wife had a dangerous run-in with a fuzzy caterpillar when she was twenty-eight weeks pregnant. That's right . . . a caterpillar. Actually, it was one of the most poisonous caterpillars in the world.

I was standing at an organization fair at Spartanburg Methodist College talking to a freshman when I received a frantic call from my wife, Elizabeth. I could barely comprehend what she was saying because she was in tears, clearly panicking.

"Chad, I'm scared that I'm going into pre-term labor," she cried into the phone. "I—I'm at a park. This caterpillar stung me on both legs, and then I could feel the venom working its way up my legs. The intense pain has traveled to my chest. Now I'm having contractions. I'm scared I'm going to have trouble breathing. What should I do?"

I didn't hesitate to say, "Call 911 right now. Where's Wyatt?" Wyatt was just two at the time.

"He's playing on the swing set. There's a nice woman here with her child. I just met her, but she's watching Wyatt right now. You're on the other side of town. How will you get here in time?" Elizabeth asked.

"Don't worry about that. Just call an ambulance," I answered. "I'll see if someone on that side of town can come pick up Wyatt."

I hung up and quickly dialed my boss, John Lancaster, while Elizabeth called 911. John fortunately was near the park. He picked up Wyatt while an ambulance picked up my panicking wife.

The paramedics told my wife, "Elizabeth, you need to relax. The more upset you are, the faster the poison will travel through your body and your baby's." That wasn't comforting. The paramedics rushed her to the emergency room, and by the time I arrived at the hospital, Elizabeth had been admitted.

When I got there and asked her whereabouts, the lady at the reception desk in the lobby said, "Oh, you're the husband of the caterpillar woman. We heard about her."

That's what the doctors and nurses called Elizabeth for the rest of her pregnancy. Hospital workers would enter her room and say, "I have nothing to do with your care, but I just have to see your caterpillar." The kind woman at the playground captured it and gave it to the 911 responders so they could identify it. Word had spread, and all sorts of people came see the caterpillar that had hospitalized my wife.

Elizabeth, being only twenty-eight weeks pregnant, clearly was not ready to meet our son Clark yet, and neither were the doctors. They administered medications to stop the contractions, but it still took twenty-four hours before the contractions ceased. Only then could Elizabeth be released from the hospital. She spent the last nine weeks of her pregnancy on bedrest and had to be readmitted one other time because of strong, early contractions. Clark did arrive a little early, but fortunately he was completely healthy.

When Elizabeth and I got home from her initial hospital stay, we did research and determined that she had been bitten a "puss caterpillar." Writer David Pegg wrote an article about the world's most dangerous insects and described the puss caterpillar like this:

> Although they look cute and furry, and even supposedly derived their name from their resemblance to "pussy cats," do not be deceived. Their fur hides spines that can cause an extremely painful reaction upon contact with human skin and sometimes chest pain, numbness, or difficulty breathing.[1]

Yes, that about sums it up. The caterpillar at first glance looked fluffy, cute, and harmless. Yet it almost changed our lives in a cat-astrophic way. We are so thankful for modern medicine and ways to stop contractions.

When I think about it, the poison that Elizabeth experienced resembles a poison that has threatened mankind since creation. I won't delve too deeply into it here because we'll explore what the Bible says about the origin of evil in Chapter Ten, but author Sally Lloyd-Jones describes the poison we face as "The Terrible Lie." In her book, *The Jesus Storybook Bible*, Lloyd-Jones describes her interpretation of the interaction between Eve and the serpent in the Garden of Eden:

> As soon as the snake saw his chance, he slithered silently up to Eve. "Does God really love you?" the serpent whispered. "If he does, why won't he let you eat the nice, juicy, delicious fruit? Poor you, perhaps God doesn't want you to be happy."

The snake's words hissed into her ears and sunk down deep into her heart, like poison. *Does God love me?* Eve wondered. Suddenly she didn't know anymore.

"Just trust me," the serpent whispered. "You don't need God. One small taste, that's all, and you'll be happier than you could ever dream . . ."

Eve picked the fruit and ate some. And Adam ate some, too. And a terrible lie came into the world. It would never leave. It would live on in every human heart, whispering to every one of God's children: "God doesn't love me."[2]

When you think about the world around you, do you believe the world has been infected by the poisonous words from the serpent? Have you ever struggled to believe that God loves you? I sure have.

I believe Jones' depiction of sin entering the world is pretty accurate, and that's why it's critical that followers of Christ spend time daily getting to know God. Does it seem odd that you can get to know God like any other person by simply spending time with him? The concept of spending time with God seemed foreign to me until I actually did just that while I was in college. I discovered that God *is* personal, and he wants us to get to know him intimately as a parent knows their child.

Spending Time with Daddy's Girl

Earlier this summer, Elizabeth had to have major back surgery. Elizabeth's parents offered to watch our six-year-old Evelyn after surgery so I could focus on being a good caregiver for Elizabeth, and we took them up on their offer.

Perhaps I should explain that Evelyn is a daddy's girl. I usually read books to her at night before bedtime, and we're very close. The grandparents live five hours away from us. At first, we thought Evelyn would only stay with them for a week. Elizabeth's recovery was more difficult than we anticipated, however, and one week turned into several.

When Elizabeth's parents finally brought Evelyn home, we were so excited to have her back. She curled up with me on our living room recliner that evening to resume our book-reading tradition. It's hard to describe in words, but I didn't quite feel as close to her as I did a few weeks earlier. She was still my child whom I loved dearly, but we temporarily lost some of the intimacy that we had as a daddy and daddy's girl. The closeness returned quickly, but only after we spent time together playing games and reading books.

Our relationship with God is like this. When we take time daily to pray and to study the Bible, we feel close to God. But when we go a day or two without thinking about him or talking to him, we lose that intimacy. He still loves us just as much—just like I still loved Evelyn when she left to visit her grandparents, and he desires to regain that intimacy with us.

God speaks to us by his Spirit in two primary ways—through prayer and through the Bible. God sometimes also uses his Spirit to speak to us through other followers of Christ and our circum- stances, but prayer and the Bible are the two main ways God com- municates with us. I want to focus on prayer in Chapter Five, so we can discuss the importance of studying the Bible in this chapter. Bible study is absolutely essential for someone who desires to get to know and love God.

By reading and understanding what God says about himself in the Bible, we can replace the "terrible lie" with what's true about God, his promises, and his plans for our lives. Also, when we under- stand the value of Christ, as we talked about in the previous chapter, it becomes easier to walk away from our counterfeit pearls so we can love God even more.

Erica's Bible Study

Erica Peterson is a Coastal Carolina University student who helped me to launch a campus ministry there a couple of years ago. She is a young lady who is passionate about studying the Bible. Here's what she said about her spiritual journey and how the Bible transformed her life:

> I look back on my years in college and I think about three special words: God is faithful. He's been with me through the valleys of my life and on the mountaintops and times of celebration. I remember my sophomore year of college, there was this certain guy that I met in a campus ministry who wanted to date me. He was cute and loved to run (running is one of my biggest passions), and he loved sports just as much as I did. But something was missing.
>
> For months he flirted with me, texted me, called me, and did his best to put himself in my life. I did think he was cute, and I absolutely loved that he enjoyed the things I enjoyed. However, soon I began to pinpoint the main reason why I felt the Lord leading me away from dating this certain guy. As I studied God's Word, it became clearer to me that the main reason that God was leading me away from him was because I did not see his passion and love for Jesus. He did a lot of good things and enjoyed the same hobbies that I enjoyed. Yet the most important aspect was not there.
>
> At this time in college, and even the years after that, all of my friends were dating someone. I felt pressured to let this guy that liked me into my life just so I could fit in with my friends who were dating people. God's words in the Bible gave me both the conviction and the courage I needed at that time. If it was not going to go

anywhere that was honoring to the Lord, we did not need to begin a relationship with one another.

Now I am a senior in college and want nothing more than to serve the Lord and to discover the height, depth, length, and width of His love. I know I wouldn't be where I'm at now if I hadn't studied God's Word and applied what he was teaching me about healthy relationships and about waiting on his provision. I continue to trust what he says in Isaiah 43:19: "Look, I am about to do something new; even now it is coming. Do you not see it? Indeed, I will make a way in the wilderness, rivers in the desert" (HCSB).

Like Erica, we need to study the Bible on a regular basis if we want to really know and love God. When I was in college, Chris and Jen Lipp, who were mentors to me, taught me an easy way to study the Bible. They called it "water skiing, snorkeling, and scuba diving in God's Word." Because it was easy for me to understand, I began using this method. Even now, many years later and after taking two seminary classes on studying the Bible, I still basically "water ski, snorkel, and scuba dive" because it's an easy method to remember.

Water Skiing, Snorkeling, and Scuba Diving

Just as water skis skim across the water, water skiing involves taking a bird's-eye view of the book of the Bible I desire to study. First, I'll take a day or two to familiarize myself with the book. In my study Bible, the introduction at the beginning of each book gives a background and overview. A commentary gives additional insight.

Fortunately, many great commentaries can be found on the Internet for free. For instance, if one wished to study the book of Philippians, a web search for "Philippians Commentary" or "the context of Philippians" will provide many resources to help give a bird's-eye view of the book.

Understanding the context of each book is critical. If one doesn't know the context, one can easily miss out on what the author of the book was really saying, and hence, what God was communicating through it. This can lead us to take verses of the Bible completely out of context.

For example, several years ago I befriended a college student named Martin in Slovakia while I was on a summer mission trip there. We spent a few weeks hanging out and getting to know each other, and one day I asked Martin what he believed about God.

"Well, of course I believe in Jesus and God," Martin said. "I believe God created us to be with him eternally in heaven."

"Really?" I asked. I started to get my hopes up that I had found a follower of Christ practically on the other side of the world. "How do you believe one gets to heaven?"

Martin replied, "One makes it to heaven by doing good works, just as it says in the Bible in James 2:26. 'Faith without works is dead'" (HCSB).

I understood why Martin, if he only read that one verse, thought James 2:26 said that good works can get us into heaven, but when one takes into consideration the context, he or she can see that it's not saying this at all.

The book of James was written to those who were already believers, many of whom already had faith and had already begun an eternal life with God. The author was calling out to believers who weren't living out their faith daily and challenging them to be doers and not just hearers of the word.

Because I had spent a considerable amount of time building a friendship with Martin, I felt comfortable trying to reason with him without arguing. I tried convincing him that faith (not works) leads to our salvation by sharing Ephesians 2:8–9 with him: "For by grace you have been saved through faith. And this not your own doing; it is the gift of God, not a result of works, so that no one may boast."

I also used an example of Jesus and the thief on the cross. Because the thief demonstrated that he had faith in him, Jesus told him, "Truly, I say to you, today you will be with me in Paradise" (Luke 23:43). I explained to Martin that the thief didn't have time to do anything good before he died a few minutes later, that it was his faith that led to his salvation, but Martin refused to believe.

Martin was so fixated on what that one verse said that he failed to see the context surrounding the verse. We must understand the context surrounding each book of the Bible so that we don't miss the author's intended meaning. The main questions to ask while water skiing are these:

Who wrote it?
For whom was it written?
When was it written?
What were the circumstances?
From where was it written?
What is the purpose of this letter/book?

Knowing the answers to these fairly simple questions will allow a better understanding of any book of the Bible. For shorter books such as Paul's letter to the Philippians, reading the entire book in one sitting helps in understanding the context.

Snorkeling involves getting a little bit deeper. If water skiing is getting a bird's-eye view, then snorkeling is getting just a little bit further in. One can see below the surface from this vantage point, but we still aren't diving in completely. This involves getting a good view of what's in each chapter. Snorkeling is more academic and involves understanding the structure of the book we're studying. It can lead to a greater understanding of the meaning of the text.

To snorkel through a chapter, one diagrams each chapter before getting deeper and scuba diving through it. This sounds harder than it actually is. For example, when I snorkeled through the first chapter of Philippians, I read through the chapter a couple of times and found that it was laid out in five major parts: 1) Greetings, 2) Paul's thanksgiving, 3) Paul's imprisonment has advanced the gospel, 4) To live is Christ, and 5) Paul's encouragement to walk worthy of the gospel.

One doesn't have to take Bible classes or have a seminary degree to study and understand the Bible. In fact, the Bible teaches that all believers have the Holy Spirit in their lives, and the Spirit helps us to understand each passage we read.

College students and many young adults keep hectic schedules and might not have time to do an in-depth Bible study every day. Don't beat yourself up if you fall into this category. The important thing is that a person is reading the Bible regularly and that the context of the Scripture being studied is understood.

As we study the Bible, we come to know God more. The more we know God, the more we love him.

Once we know the context and the overall message of a chapter, we begin to scuba dive through that chapter. Picture a scuba diver exploring the ocean floor, picking up starfish, conch shells, sand dollars, and perhaps sunken treasures. Unlike a snorkeler, a scuba diver can look at everything in detail.

Scuba diving Scripture is getting really deep in the Word. It involves looking at each phrase and word and learning how the message can apply to our everyday lives.

When I scuba dive through a chapter of the Bible, I just take each "part" or section I outlined while snorkeling and spend thirty minutes or so looking closely at it and learning how it applies to my life. I usually won't look at more than one part on the same day. That way I can focus on the next section the next time I spend time with God and his Word.

When I first scuba dove through Philippians 1:1, where Paul said, "Paul and Timothy, servants of Christ Jesus," I asked myself,

"What does it mean to be a servant of Christ? What did it mean to be a servant in Paul's day? If someone looked closely at my life, would they say I am Christ's servant?" Paul saw a servant as someone who paid close attention to his or her master. Their entire day revolved around living for their master and doing the things the master wanted them to do. In short, their life wasn't about them.

While I've never heard a sermon on Philippians 1:1, God taught me a lot when I studied that verse myself. It made me think about my life, see my shortfalls, and make a commitment to live to please myself less while living to please my Master more.

Scuba diving through the Bible, we can understand more and more about God and why we should want to live for him. For example, in the book of Jonah, God sent the prophet Jonah to the land of Nineveh to warn them what would happen if they didn't live for him.

The people of Nineveh were the most faithless people on earth, and yet, when they listened to Jonah and gave their lives over to God, he was faithful to save them. An entire city, one of the most evil cities on the planet, was saved because of God's faithfulness.

In Luke 11:32, Jesus even alluded to the fact that the people of Nineveh will be in heaven because of their faith in God. The theme of Jonah is that God is faithful even when we're not.

When we study more of the Bible, we can begin to see one big overarching theme that covers the whole Bible—God's great redemption plan for the world.

The Music of the Gospel

God's redemption plan for us is the main theme in the Bible, and every chapter and verse of the Bible ties in to this theme in some way.

There's almost an art to seeing it in every book, but with practice one can not only master seeing it but can find life in it. Bible scholar Keith Johnson has referred to the art of seeing God's redemption plan throughout the Bible as "hearing the music of the gospel." Johnson writes:

> Imagine yourself in a large house in which those who are deaf and those who can hear are living together. In one of the rooms, you see a guy sitting in a chair and listening to music on his iPod. Rhythmically, he's tapping his foot, drumming his thighs, jutting his chin out, swaying to the beat, and pursing his lips like Mick Jagger or someone. His entire body moves in response to what his ears are hearing. It's obvious that he's enjoying himself and listening to a pretty good song.
>
> A few minutes later, one of the deaf persons enters the room. Seeing the guy listening to the music and impersonating Mick Jagger, he thinks, That looks like fun. I think I'll try that. So he sits down next to him and begins to imitate him. Awkwardly at first, he tries drumming his thighs, jutting his chin out, and swaying to the music just like the guy with the iPod. With a little practice, he begins to catch on to it. By watching and trying, he begins to mirror the other guy's actions pretty closely. But although he eventually gets better at keeping time, he concludes that it's not as much fun or as easy as it initially seemed (especially the chin jut—very difficult to do when you're not actually hearing the music).
>
> After a while, a third person enters the room and watches this scene. What does he see? Two people apparently doing the same thing, apparently listening to the same thing. Is there a difference? Absolutely. The first guy hears the music and his actions are a natural response to the music's rhythm and melody. The second guy is merely imitating the outward actions. Being deaf, he's not listening to anything.[3]

According to Johnson, the first guy is like someone who reads the Bible and "hears the music of the gospel" throughout the passages he or she reads. The second guy, the one who is deaf but imitates the first guy, is like someone who doesn't see God's redemption plan unfolding throughout the Bible. The second guy goes through the motions but doesn't enjoy it and isn't too interesting to watch, either.

Jesus doesn't use the term "hearing the music of the gospel," but he said something similar in Luke 18:10–14, in his parable of the Pharisee and tax collector:

> Two men went up into the temple to pray, one a
> Pharisee and the other a tax collector. The Pharisee,
> standing by himself, prayed thus: "God, I thank you that
> I am not like other men, extortioners, unjust, adulterers,
> or even like this tax collector. I fast twice a week; I give
> tithes of all that I get." But the tax collector, standing far
> off, would not even lift up his eyes to heaven, but beat
> his breast, saying, "God, be merciful to me, a sinner!"
> I tell you, this man went down to his house justified,
> rather than the other. For everyone who exalts himself
> will be humbled, but the one who humbles himself will
> be exalted.

The Pharisees, who were legalistic, went through the motions, but they never understood the gospel. The tax collector, like many of the "sinners" that hung out with Jesus and followed him, got it. They heard the music of the gospel and responded to it with repentance and thankfulness. Like the younger son in the parable of the lost sons, they recognized the depth of their sin and their need for a Savior.

From Genesis to Revelation, the Bible does two things: 1) exposes our brokenness, and 2) points us to our Savior.

That's the gospel—the good news that God had a plan from the beginning to rescue his children and bring us back to himself. No matter how unfaithful we are to God, he faithfully pursues us so that we can have complete joy in him eternally.

As I've studied the Bible throughout the years, I've slowly but surely learned to hear the music of the gospel throughout Scripture. If you need help learning to hear it, go to my website, www.findingauthenticchristianity.com, and study a book of the Bible using devotionals I've posted. When you visit the site, click on the "Quiet Times" icon. There you'll find devotionals for the many books of the Bible I've walked through so far on that website.

This morning, after "water skiing and snorkeling" through 1 Kings for a couple of days, I began to scuba dive deeper and found the jewel I shared in my devotional posted below. See if you can hear the music of the gospel in the following devotional.

1 Kings 1 Devotional—"We All Want to Be King"

There's a part of all of us that wants to be in control of our circumstances, and when we lose control, we get angry or frustrated. One morning about six months ago, as I was driving to work in my car, I turned off the radio to pray. I prayed, "Lord, I surrender my heart and my attitude to you today," and then someone pulled out right in front of me, almost causing an accident. In the middle of my prayer, I yelled toward my windshield, "You idiot! What are you doing?"

Someone had taken away my control, and it made me angry. Realizing I had just lost my temper and that I had taken control of my attitude away from God, I then prayed, "Oops, I'm sorry, Lord. I confess that my attitude just then did not reflect your kindness and self-control. Once again, I invite you to take control over my heart and my attitude." How often we forget to live a life surrendered to Jesus!

In 1 Kings 1, David was at the end of his life, and one of his sons tried to take control of the throne against David's wishes: "Now Adonijah the son of Haggith exalted himself, saying, 'I will be king.' And he prepared for himself chariots and horsemen, and fifty men to run before him" (1:5).

When I first read this, I became frustrated with Adonijah for trying to mess up God's plan to have Solomon be the king of Israel. However, the more I thought about it, the more I realized that I'm like Adonijah. God has a plan for me to be pure and to reflect his love and bear his fruit. However, so many times, like that morning in the car, I fail to surrender my heart and attitude to God.

When we surrender our lives to God, he brings us into his eternal kingdom where Christ is King. Our new reality is that we can no longer be kings of our own lives. We can no longer just do whatever we want to do. Our lives belong to Jesus, and if we allow him to do in us what he wants to do, the great thing is that he has a life in store for us that's so much better than we imagined.

Spend some time reflecting on ways that you try to be the king of your own kingdom. Confess any sin God brings to your mind, and surrender your heart and attitude to Christ, allowing him to be the King of your life. God has a life that's so much better for us than when we try to be king of our own lives. Let's allow Jesus to be the King he was meant to be.

Parting Thoughts about Loving God with All Our Hearts

Could you "hear the music of the gospel" in my devotional on 1 Kings 1? There's something about God's great redemption plan for the world that draws me to fall in love with Jesus. I don't deserve him. Yet, despite what I deserve, he adopted me into his family.

But there's more to loving God than just loving him with our hearts. A husband can love his wife and still be unfaithful to her.

A child can love his or her parents and still be disobedient. God required more of us than just our affection when he gave the Great Commandment to "love the Lord your God with all your heart and with all your soul and with all your mind." He required devotion, and that's what we'll explore in the next several chapters.

Notes

[1]David Pegg, "25 Most Dangerous Bugs in the World," List25, July 15, 2013, http://list25.com/25-most-dangerous-insects-in-the-world/.

[2]Sally Lloyd-Jones, *The Jesus Storybook Bible: Every Story Whispers His Name* (Grand Rapids: Zonderkids, 2007), 30.

[3]Keith Johnson, "Hearing the Music of the Gospel," CruPress, accessed September 28, 2015, http://crupressgreen.com/wp-content/uploads/2012/02 /Music_of_the_Gospel.pdf.

Part 2

All Your Soul

"The heart can think
of no devotion
Greater than being
shore to the ocean—
Holding the curve of one position,
Counting an endless repetition."

—Robert Frost

CHAPTER ~5~

I Will Go Where You Want Me to Go

Transitions can be tough. moving is hard. Even the physical task of moving all the heavy furniture is daunting, especially since my knees aren't the best. Three years ago, Elizabeth and I were preparing to move from South Carolina to Georgia in order for me to take a national role in our campus ministry. At a gathering of friends a couple of nights before we left Charleston, my good friend Mark Andrews shared a fictional story with me that encouraged and yet challenged me at the same time:

> One day God told one of his followers to climb a giant ladder. The man climbed and climbed the ladder, which seemed to go up forever. He became afraid, and suddenly God said, "Don't be afraid. I'm right here with you to keep you safe."

The man continued to climb until the ladder went up into a cloud and stopped. When the man reached the top, he saw a plank that went out from the ladder over the edge of the cloud. God said, "I want you to go out to the end of the plank." Reluctantly, the man slowly walked out to the end of the plank.

When the man reached the end of the plank, God said, "I want you to jump."

The man looked down, and he could barely make out what looked like a small, empty pool down below. "But God," the man replied. "I don't even know if I'll land in the pool, and even if I do, I won't survive. There's no water in the pool."

God said, "I want you to jump . . . and then I'm going to fill it."

This simple story is a great description of faith. Sometimes God asks us to do things that we can never do on our own. Sometimes taking a step of faith can seem like jumping off a cloud into a pool with no water. Sometimes before we jump, after we jump, and as we're falling, we're scared and we question God.

That's the way my first month in Atlanta was for me.

Back in Charleston, we struggled to sell our house. Finally, after months of showings and price reductions, a buyer made a reasonable offer. The night before the home inspection, Elizabeth's parents checked on the house. All was well.

The next morning, much to everyone's shock, the inspector found that a pipe inside a wall had burst and flooded the house. Fortunately, our insurance company came through and covered nearly ten thousand dollars in damages.

Our dear friend and contractor, Chris Brace, worked late nights replacing flooring, cabinets, and walls and fixed everything just before closing. There certainly were some stressful moments during those few weeks.

On the Atlanta side of the move, our closing date on the new house and the kids' start date for school didn't line up well; so we moved our family into an extended-stay hotel. The hotel looked safe enough in the pictures online.

But not everything is as it appears on the Internet. We arrived late on a Sunday night and could immediately tell we were in for a trial. We walked into the first room assigned to us and found that housekeeping hadn't cleaned it. The kids looked around and said, "This is Atlanta?" A trip to the front desk later, we had a key for another room.

The second room smelled moldy, but exhausted from a long day of travel, we decided to get the kids settled anyway. After setting up our Pack 'n Play for Josilynn, we arranged three sleeping bags on the floor beside our bed.

I couldn't sleep that night.

The sounds upstairs were strange. For a while, we could hear what sounded like two people running in place on opposite sides of the room. Then one of the pairs of feet would suddenly run across the room to the other side. From midnight until 6 A.M., the pattering of feet never stopped.

The next day, Elizabeth headed out to take the kids to their first day of school, and I went to our office to meet my new coworkers. All day long, I kept thinking of the story Mark shared with me.

We had taken a leap of faith. We prayed all day long hoping to hear that we would close on our house early, but we never received the positive news from our real estate agent.

Elizabeth communicated to me that night after we put the kids to bed that she felt unsafe. There were a lot of single men staying at the hotel, and they watched her and our girls when Elizabeth went back and forth from our room to the car.

Along with that we had an ant problem in our room, and the strange noises in the room above us continued that night. We decided to begin looking for a new home base.

Then on Tuesday, a phone call put us over the edge.

The caller was our real estate agent, who told us our contract on our new house was likely to fall through due to a big mistake by our lending broker. "All I can tell you is to pray," our agent said. "In all my years as a real estate agent, I've never seen such a blunder made by a bank. It doesn't look good, and the seller said the deal is off."

I spent the next few hours praying with some of my new coworkers. "*Lord, I've jumped toward the pool by following your calling and moving my family to Atlanta, but there's no water in the pool. Please, please fill the pool.*"

Later that day, God "filled our pool." Our real estate agent called with the wonderful news that the seller of our house had a change of heart that afternoon (while we were praying). The closing was back on the schedule for the next week.

Meanwhile, a coworker invited our family to move into their basement until we closed on our house, and we were able to get out of the hotel that felt so unsafe.

In what ways have you taken a leap of faith into an unfilled pool? Are you praying to God, trusting in him to fill the pool?

We should have ongoing answers to the two questions above. When I first placed my faith in Christ many years ago, I had a misconception that becoming a follower of Christ involved taking one giant leap of faith by surrendering my heart to God. Now I realize that surrendering to God's will is a daily endeavor. Each day I'm faced with a choice of either doing things my way or surrendering to the will of God.

The concept of surrendering our lives to the will of God daily is related to our devotion to God. When Jesus commands us to love God with all of our souls in Matthew 22:37, he is talking about devotion.

Five parts of our lives are related to our devotion to God: our feet, our hands, our thoughts, our mouths, and our finances. To fully surrender our hearts to Jesus, we must go where God wants us to go, do what he wants us to do (which also includes what we think about), say what he wants us to say, and give what he wants us to give.

If we can learn to surrender all five areas to God, we can live a life fully devoted to him. Don't get discouraged or overwhelmed if you read through these next few chapters and realize you have a long way to go, though. We're all in process, and spiritual growth requires intentionality over time. If you are intentional and make an effort to get to know God better, you'll look back several years from now and realize you've come a long way.

My story of our move to Atlanta is one example of how I felt led by God to go someplace, but I can think of many other examples of how God has led me to go places on at least a monthly, if not a weekly, basis.

One recent example occurred as I read the church bulletin one Sunday morning. It described an opportunity for members of the church to serve dinner to a couple hundred residents of a nursing home in a poor part of town. As I was reading the bulletin, I thought to myself, *I really need to do this with my boys, Wyatt and Clark.*

Now it's possible that I just came up with that thought myself, but to me it doesn't seem likely because I know myself. There were many other things I could have done with my time other than spending an entire evening and most of a night serving dinner at an event. I would have loved to spend that time with my family. I don't think I would have come up with the idea to serve others on that special day without help from God.

Wyatt, Clark, and I attended the event and fed a couple hundred people Christmas dinner. The elderly men and women (especially the women) just loved Wyatt and Clark. They all seemed genuinely thankful that we chose to spend the night volunteering to serve them. But I don't think the people from the nursing home were as impacted as we were.

For the rest of the Christmas break, my boys reflected on the joy they received while serving. Afterward, Clark said, "You know what, Dad? I think we need to do that more often, and we definitely need to do it again next year."

I believe the thought that we needed to go to the nursing home came from the Lord, and if we take the time to pray and to listen to God, he will lead us to go places on an ongoing basis.

Taking Time to Pray

We all know that we should pray. The Bible commands us to do it, and every time we think of praying most of us are probably convicted that we don't pray enough.

The Bible also clearly states that God answers prayer: "Ask, and it will be given to you; seek, and you will find; knock, and it will be opened to you. For everyone who asks receives, and the one who seeks finds, and to the one who knocks it will be opened" (Matt. 7:7–8).

So if God answers when we pray, why don't we pray more?

There are many answers to this question. Some would say we're too distracted, which is true. Others might say we're too guilty from our sinful habits, and talking with God makes us feel more guilt. Still, others might say we have too many other priorities, our schedules are too full, or "I sure don't want to be so heavenly minded that I am no earthly good."

Too many have been taught from the earliest days in church and Sunday school that "we must do tasks for God and keep doing them as much as we can. God would rather have me doing good things rather than wasting time in prayer."

The root of all of these answers is that we don't have enough faith in God. We either forget that God is with us at all times and wants to communicate with us, or we don't have faith that he cares enough about us or our problems to help.

The good news is that God knows we struggle with our faith, and he's ready to meet us right where we are. He even said all we need is just a little bit of faith, and he will move mountains for us. "For truly, I say to you, if you have faith like a grain of mustard seed, you will say to this mountain, 'Move from here to there,' and it will move, and nothing will be impossible for you" (Matt. 17:20).

Recently Elizabeth and I saw God do something amazing right before our eyes after Elizabeth met some new friends, Lucas and Marie, at the pool. They're an interracial couple from France, and our biracial daughter Josilynn immediately became friends with their daughter. We also discovered that their two oldest boys were friends with our son and daughter at school.

Marie shared with Elizabeth that she was recently diagnosed with breast cancer and that she would be having major surgery over the summer to remove the tumors. After Marie's surgery, Elizabeth rallied our friends in our church and our neighborhood to provide meals for them. Someone delivered dinner to Lucas and Marie nearly every night for over a month. Not only were we organizing meals for Lucas and Marie and checking up on them regularly, but we also took time to pray for both of them constantly during this time.

Lucas and Marie were overwhelmed by the love shown to them. Late one Saturday night shortly after Marie's surgery, we received a text from Lucas saying that he was bringing his kids to our church. "We want to see everyone who visited us and to thank them for their kindness," Lucas said.

The next morning, Lucas, his kids, and Marie's mother, who was visiting from France, visited our church. Afterward, Marie's mom showered us with kisses and hugs, thanking us again and again for caring for her daughter. She didn't speak English, but she thanked us in French while Lucas translated. She went home and told Marie she needed to visit our church because the people were so wonderful.

We continued to pray for their family, and when Marie felt better, Lucas and Marie brought their family to our church every Sunday for the next couple of months. We had some spiritual conversations with them, but we couldn't tell if they had faith in Christ.

Then we were crushed to hear that they were moving to Palm Beach, Florida. How could this be? They seemed so close to believing in Christ. How could God move them away at what seemed to be such a critical time in their spiritual lives? Would they ever truly receive Christ as their Lord?

Well, we did have a little bit of faith that God would still move in their lives, and we prayed for them as they left. Recently, Marie returned to Atlanta for a few days to receive her chemotherapy treatment for her cancer, and she spent an afternoon with Elizabeth at our house. This is what Marie told Elizabeth:

> We've found a wonderful church in Palm Beach. I did
> not know that my cousin went to church, and he invited
> us. We loved the church here, so we knew we just had to
> visit. The pastor is such a strong, lively teacher, and his
> sermons keep our attention. We'll go again for sure.
>
> You know, many people say that cancer is so bad,
> but it hasn't been so bad for me. It's actually been really
> good for me and for my family. Our first year in Atlanta
> was depressing. We didn't have any friends, and we
> weren't very happy. If it weren't for my cancer, I would
> have never met so many wonderful friends and would

have never attended your church. For me, cancer has
made my life better.

God is still very much involved in the lives of Lucas and Marie,
and we continue to pray for them. God cares about them and is
with them everywhere they go. This is just another example that
God cares about us, and he listens to our prayers. All we need is
just a little bit of faith, the faith of a mustard seed, and he's ready
to move mountains for us.

We all have people like Lucas and Marie around us. Even when
we don't have compassion for them, God does. That's why he has
placed people like us around them with just enough faith to pray
and show them who God is.

Can you think of someone around you who has a need for
prayer or an act of love and kindness? Have you prayed for them?

Now is a good time to begin praying for the people God has
placed around us. It may be that we're the only person in their
lives who knows Christ, and we may be the one God has chosen
to introduce them to him.

As you begin praying for those near to you, be aware going into
it that God requires more than just our prayers. He will lead us to
be involved in their lives, and if we will surrender to go where he
wants us to go, he just might use us to be part of something amazing.

Don't Just Pray for God's Will

Years ago, right after I went into full-time college ministry, I
attended a conference with more than a thousand college students
in Greensboro, North Carolina. Tommy Nelson, who was then the
pastor of Denton Bible Church in Denton, Texas, was the main
speaker. I remember sitting in the auditorium during one of his
talks. My mind was wandering a bit. But then Tommy said something that grabbed my attention.

He said, "Don't just spend your whole life praying and asking God to show you his will for your life."

I immediately sat up in my seat and thought, *Surely he didn't just tell us not to pray, did he?*

Tommy then repeated, "Don't just spend your whole life praying and asking God to show you his will for your life. Pray according to James 1:5. Then lift up your eyes and look around. Find out where God is moving. Get in the middle of it. Then you'll be right in the middle of God's will."

I'll never forget how those words impacted my life. My perspective on prayer changed that day, and my prayer life continues to be impacted by his words.

What Tommy Nelson was saying is that our intimacy with God involves both praying and going. It's not enough just to pray, and it's not enough just to go.

God is at work all around us, and while we pray, we must constantly look around to see where he is at work so that we can get in the middle of it. I've heard others say that our default should be to go, and we should pray and ask God to close the door if it's not in his will for us to go.

This summer as I was spending time praying daily, I sensed that I should spend more time with my twelve-year-old, Wyatt, as he transitions into his teenage years. For years, I've been praying for Wyatt's sexual purity. I decided to go on a weekend retreat with him to talk about what the Bible says about how to remain sexually pure in both our thoughts and actions.

We had an amazing weekend together in the mountains, fishing, playing paintball, and talking about sexual purity. It would have been awkward and probably was at first, but the fishing and paintball helped to create a fun, safe environment to talk.

After the trip, I sensed during a prayer time that I needed to get to know Wyatt's friends and be more involved in his life. Lifting up my eyes, as Tommy Nelson said, I found an opportunity to serve in our student ministry at church. I volunteered to help out, and now I speak weekly to about seventy or eighty preteens and teenagers and lead a weekly junior high Bible study. I've already gotten to know many of the friends Wyatt spends his free time with.

It's been a joy and honor to have an opportunity to help shape the lives of a room full of crazy teens and preteens. At first, I didn't want to lead an eighth-grade Bible study because I've had a fear of junior high kids that started when I was one of them.

Once again, God knew what was best.

I've found real joy in being a part of their lives. Had I not spent time in daily prayer this summer and then looked around to find where God was moving, I would have missed out on the joy of being in the center of God's will.

I asked two of my friends to share their story of going where God wanted them to go. Matt and Sabrina Pursley were students at Lenoir-Rhyne University when I recruited them to help me lead a summer mission trip a few years ago. They became such close friends that I recruited them to go into college ministry full-time after they completed college. I tried getting them to join a ministry team I was leading at the time in Charleston, South Carolina, but God had other plans.

Matt and Sabrina's Story

Two years ago, Matt and Sabrina were at new-staff training for Cru, a ministry for college students and faculty, when they sensed God was calling them somewhere they never thought they'd go. This is what Matt said about their experience:

> The week was here. The week so many weeks had
> been building up to. My wife Sabrina and I had joined
> staff with Cru and were in prayerful anticipation of
> where God was going to send us. We were open to

go anywhere, or so we thought. One night we prayed together asking God to send us where he wanted us. Except my prayer had a tagline, "God I'll go wherever you want me to go . . . just not New York City." I grew up in the South. New York City was a place full of Yankees fans and muggers. That's not somewhere I wanted to be.

Well, the next day, the need was presented and a call was made for where else but the Big Apple. Even more specifically this call was for Destino, the contextually Latino ministry of Cru. Now the contextualization I could get on board with. I was, after all, bilingual in English and Spanish, had minored in Spanish, was fairly well cultured, and even spent a little time overseas, but the New York City part of this call, well, that was a whole other fear factor.

As the next few days and even weeks went on, my wife and I prayed hard, asking God if this was really where he wanted us to be. Thanks to some wise counsel and generosity, we were able take a trip to the city and see firsthand what ministry with Destino would look like. As soon as I stepped off the plane, my heart began to change.

With every step I took (which is a lot in the city), I saw a new face, a different skin color, millions of different people who each are made in the image of God, but most have no idea who he is. Then I very clearly heard, "And how are they to believe in him of whom they have never heard? And how are they to hear without someone preaching?" (Rom. 10:14) It was very clear that God was calling us to the city. And so we went.

We now live in Washington Heights, which is a neighborhood in uptown Manhattan. Our time here has not been easy. We've had our apartment broken into, had a cockroach infestation, seen someone pull a knife on another person, and been woken up by people outside screaming for help, to name a few struggles. Many times I've asked God why he wants us here. It has been challenging in ways that I've never experienced before, and many times it has been exhausting. But he's a good God. He's spoken through his Word and he does not overlook his beloved. He is faithful. And since he is faithful, we can be faithful.

In all of our challenges, pains, and sufferings God has allowed us to experience him in a way that I never have before. He's shown us that we're receiving an eternal glory (2 Cor. 4:16–20), that being in his will is the safest place to be (Ps. 4:8), and that he is our Great High Priest who sympathizes with us and helps us (Heb. 4:14–16). And he's shown us that he's worthy.

Going Where God Wants Us to Go

In Chapter Three, we explored the parable of the pearl of great value. The point was made that the pearl merchant sold all of his possessions in order to attain the one pearl that was worth more than everything he had. One of the conclusions from the parable was that worship should cost us something, and as you can see in Matt and Sabrina's story, their cost has been great.

In order to be willing to go where God wants us to go, we will have to make sacrifices. We might have to sacrifice our career or a relationship that's not going in the direction that God is leading us, and we might even have to sacrifice some of our hopes and dreams. It's not going to be easy to go where God wants us to go, but the cool thing is that, as we take steps of faith, God will change the desires of our hearts to match his will.

Before Elizabeth and I made the move from Charleston to Atlanta that I shared earlier, we absolutely loved Charleston and said we never wanted to move. When we sensed God calling us to make the move, at first we weren't excited about moving to the big city. Elizabeth even cried a few times right before we moved because she knew we would miss our family and friends in Charleston.

Now we love Atlanta!

We've gotten involved in a wonderful church. Our kids are thriving in school, and we've made some truly close friends. We literally thank God every day for moving us to this great city.

I find comfort in God's promise to his people in Jeremiah 29:11: "'For I know the plans I have for you,' declares the LORD, 'plans to prosper you and not to harm you, plans to give you a hope and a future'" (NIV1984).

Prayer has always given us the open window to hear and follow God's plan for us. We have found that prayer is a major factor in opening ourselves to following God's path for us.

In the next few chapters, we'll continue to explore what it means to surrender different areas of our lives so that we can love God with all of our souls. At the end of Chapter Eight, there will be an opportunity to take a Surrender Pledge, a meaningful pledge between you and the Lord that could change the trajectory of your life. Let's explore the next area of surrendering, which involves doing what God wants us to do.

CHAPTER ~6~

I Will Do What You Want Me to Do

"Chad, if you ever see lightning or hear thunder, drive this aluminum boat immediately to land and get out."

Those seem like wise words that should be obvious to follow, don't they? Well, unfortunately for an indestructible sixteen-year-old, those words weren't obvious enough. Failing to follow that one simple rule nearly cost me my life.

Actually, I find myself saying that phrase "nearly cost me my life" so often I really thank God that I'm alive today.

The morning I embarked on my first boating trip without my father began as a beautiful sunny day. My friend Jamie and I drove my dad's boat out to Lake Harding, located on the Alabama-Georgia state line. We anchored at my favorite spot for catfish near the marina and caught several fish before a huge storm came out of nowhere.

As the rain started to come down, the fish began to bite like I'd never experienced on the lake before. I remembered my dad's words, but as it began to thunder all around us, I kept rationalizing that it would be okay to catch a few more before heading to the dock.

After all, the dock wasn't that far away. Or so I thought.

Meanwhile, my mother stood at the kitchen sink looking out the window at the stormy sky and became worried. That was before cell phones were affordable, so calling us was impossible. When the storm grew stronger and I hadn't arrived home, she dashed to her car and out to Lake Harding.

But back at the lake, the fishing was truly amazing.

The rain had picked up, and, yes, it was true that I could barely see Jamie at the front of the boat. He didn't seem to mind the rain either. The hard rain hit the water and formed a thick mist around us. I could tell he was catching as many catfish as I was because I could hear his joyful whooping and hollering.

Every time I cast my line, I felt a strong bite within seconds. I barely noticed the lightning all around or the distant voice of someone screaming my name.

Finally Jamie noticed. "Chad, is that your mom over there at the marina?" As soon as he said those words, a bolt of lightning struck the water a quarter of a mile away. I was sure I felt a small amount of electric current shoot through the boat and my body.

Suddenly, I was fully aware of the imminent danger. I squinted to see Jamie, and his fearful look showed he had felt the electricity as well. We reeled in our lines quickly, started the engine, and zipped to the marina. Moments after we stepped out of the boat, another bolt of lightning hit the water close to our fishing spot across the bay.

This true story is a clear illustration of what happens in our spiritual lives when we ignore God or don't listen to his voice.

The main theme of the Bible is God's relationship with mankind and his plan to bring the world back into a relationship with him. However, there's another purpose of the Bible that we often neglect. That purpose is to show us how we should live and respond to such a loving Father.

Think about some of the destructive behaviors you've engaged in over the years. If your life resembles mine, there are times you've done things you knew you shouldn't have been doing. Perhaps you heard the distant voice of God guiding you, but you probably ignored God's wise words, much like I ignored my father's words that day in the boat.

Listening to the wise words of God means being willing to *do* what God wants us to do—loving God with our souls.

God shows us his love by telling us through his holy Word how to live. Listening to God is showing him that we love him.

Do you think it's more important to *say* that you love someone or to *show* that you love someone? Ponder this thought.

I could *tell* my wife Elizabeth that I love her, but isn't it more important to *show* her that I love her? What if I told her every day that I loved her but was involved in an adulterous affair on the side? On the flip side, what if I *never* told her I loved her, but every day I did something to *show* her I loved her, like sending flowers, encouraging her, and being faithful?

It's good to tell someone that you love them, but it's even more important to show it.

Most of us probably are guilty of saying we love God while doing things that prove the opposite. God is still faithful, despite our unfaithfulness, but he does desire for us to show him that we love him. Before we dig in to some of the ways we can show God we love him, it's important to address one of the biggest misconceptions about Christian faith that young people have today: the misconception that living a holy life will ruin our fun and happiness.

The Joy of Being Holy

My favorite passage on happiness comes from Psalm 1, the gateway into the entire book of Psalms. It tells us that true happiness comes from living our lives by God's instruction rather than by the advice of those who reject that instruction.

> Blessed is the man who walks not in the counsel of the wicked, nor stands in the way of sinners, nor sits in the seat of scoffers; but his delight is in the law of the LORD, and on his law he meditates day and night. He is like a tree planted by streams of water that yields its fruit in its season, and its leaf does not wither. In all that he does, he prospers. The wicked are not so, but are like chaff that the wind drives away. (1:1–4)

C. S. Lewis, in his *Reflections on the Psalms*, ponders how anyone can "delight" in the law of the Lord. He writes, "Their delight in the Law is a delight in having touched firmness; like the pedestrian's delight in feeling the hard road beneath his feet after a false short cut has entangled him in muddy fields."[1] The law is good because firmness is good. I will never forget the feelings of safety, relief, and joy when I stepped out of that boat during that storm those many years ago.

Last year, my family attended a conference in Ft. Collins, Colorado, that was put on by our employer. Because we had to purchase six airplane tickets, we saved a considerable amount of money by booking a 6:00 A.M. flight out of Denver to Atlanta. Our plan was to get a few hours of sleep, wake the kids at 3:00 A.M., drive an hour to Denver, and arrive at the airport by 4:00 A.M. for our flight.

Well, things never go as planned when you have four kids, and we were lucky that we got on the road by three thirty. About halfway to the airport, Elizabeth said, "We're in great shape. We'll arrive at the airport at four thirty, in plenty of time to make our 6:00 A.M. flight. We're fine."

That's when absolute pandemonium broke out in our rented minivan.

It started with Clark, our child prone to carsickness, saying, "I don't feel so good. I think I'm going to be sick."

"Can you make it to the airport?" I asked, trying not to swerve, "We're only thirty minutes away."

Clark replied in a panicked voice, "Dad! Pull over now! Pull . . . ahhhhh!"

He then projectile vomited all over the car, spraying two-year-old Josilynn's head in front of him. Most thoughtful people might cover their mouths or at least hold still until they're done vomiting, but eight-year-olds aren't that thoughtful.

When his little sister Evelyn, who was beside him, started screaming in disgust, Clark turned toward her and vomited on her lap. He then made sure he covered his older brother, who was yelling on the other side of him. Within a few seconds, our car went from being peaceful to being out of control with four children screaming at the top of their lungs. I nearly flipped the car as I slammed on the brakes and skidded to a stop along the Interstate.

Elizabeth and I got the three older kids out and lined them up along the side of the road so they could take turns dry heaving while Elizabeth unloaded suitcases, looking for clean clothes. As if that wasn't enough, in between his dry heaving, one of my children (who will remain nameless) yelled out, "Dad! I've gotta go to the bathroom! I think I'm going to have diarrhea!" He then ran ten or fifteen yards from the side of the road toward a bush. He didn't make it!

A side note to this story is that a friend of ours named Shanda was with us in the rental van. To save money on a plane ticket, she was riding with us to the airport and then driving the car across the country to return the car to the rental company. The rental company was paying for her gas in exchange for her returning the car, but the poor girl endured the smell of vomit for the next two days as she drove home. It was embarrassing to leave her with a car that smelled so awful. Furthermore, she had gotten a glimpse of our family at one of our worst possible moments.

After we thoroughly cleaned Josilynn and the other three kids and did our best to clean the car, we finally arrived at the airport in time to sprint to our gate. Clark was wearing swim trunks and his sister's T-shirt, but we were there! Oh, how good it felt to actually get on that plane with no kids vomiting. We learned the hard way that it's not wise to fill your kids' bellies with doughnuts at 3:00 A.M. before an early morning road trip.

The psalmist's delight in the Law of the Lord is like the delight we felt when we successfully made it to the plane on time. Better yet, the psalmist's delight in Psalm 1 is like the delight we felt when we were home after that horrific trip. It felt so good to have it behind us. We had made it through a tough time and could breathe a sigh of relief. If we were hit with trials or sickness, at least we'd be safe at home to deal with it.

Being at home produces great feelings of safety.

When we're not at home, we feel more vulnerable and less safe. People don't think of living holy lives as being at home, but it is. After we give our lives to Christ, we begin to desire to be holy. As we get to know God better and love him more, our desire to be devoted to him grows. We find safety, joy, and comfort in living the way God wants us to live. That's where our "home" is.

When we don't follow God's standard for holy living, a number of things happen to us. First and foremost, as we explored in Chapter Two, we don't experience God's amazing love. He still loves us, but we don't necessarily feel his love because our fellowship with him is broken.

Second, there are consequences to our sin. Broken relationships, guilt, fear, and mistrust of God and others are just a few of the many consequences of failing to live a holy life.

And third, we don't bear the fruit of the Holy Spirit when we aren't intimate with God. Love, joy, peace, and patience are some of the fruit we grow as we live holy lives, but they wither and die when we're not living holy lives.

Living without love, joy, and peace could be compared to the suffering Shanda had to endure while she drove the rental car back from Colorado. I'm sure she longed to be home, and probably she worried that she was going to be sick from breathing in the germs.

Actually, let me compare the ease of living holy lives to the ease of trying to rid a rental car of the smell of vomit. It can seem impossible, an uphill battle. One thing I've heard some followers of Christ say over the years is that it's impossible to live a completely holy life. "No one's perfect," they say. However, the Bible is clear that while it's true everyone has failed to meet God's standard of perfection before Christ came into their life, it is possible to live a holy life with the help of God.

Holiness Is Possible

Recently I met with a young Christian man, Phil, who opened his heart to me and confessed his ongoing struggle with sexual immorality. He had a serious girlfriend and was contemplating getting engaged, but an addiction to pornography had caused problems in both his spiritual life and his relationship.

With a burdened look on his face, he said, "Chad, I just cannot obey God for even one nanosecond of my life."

"Phil," I responded, "saying holiness is out of reach for the ordinary Christian discounts the way the Bible speaks about many of the saints such as Job. Also in Luke, Zechariah and Elizabeth, John the Baptist's parents, were described as being righteous before God.

By the power of the Holy Spirit, who is in our lives and empowers us to be holy, it is *absolutely* possible to live a life that pleases God."

It's dangerous to ignore the Bible's expectation that holiness is possible. I know that for me too much emphasis on God's grace and not enough emphasis on God's truth led to an imbalance in my view of holiness early on in my Christian faith.

As I've grown in my faith, however, I've read books such as Jerry Bridges's *The Pursuit of Holiness* and Kevin DeYoung's *The Hole in Our Holiness*. Both have inspired me to live a holy life.

In his book, Kevin DeYoung writes, "There is a gap between our love for the gospel and our love for godliness. This must change. It's not pietism, legalism, or fundamentalism to take holiness seriously. It's the way of all those who have been called to a holy calling by a holy God."[2]

Being holy is about being who you were meant to be.

When God in the Bible gives the command to be holy, he's simply saying he wants you to be the real you. He wants you to be true to yourself. But the "you" he's talking about is who you are in grace, not in nature.

In other words, God doesn't want us to live the way we naturally were without Christ. He wants us to live as we truly are with Christ. "Therefore, if anyone is in Christ, he is a new creation. The old has passed away; behold, the new has come" (2 Cor. 5:17).

Ultimately, there are two things that motivate me to live a holy life.

The first is the gospel (or Jesus' acts of redemption on the cross). We talked about this when we looked at the parable of the lost sons. When we understand the depth of our sin and what Jesus did on the cross to rescue us from our sin, it motivates us to be holy.

When I'm faced with the temptation to sin, I often think to myself, *God's always been so faithful to me, even when I haven't been faithful to him. He's done so much for me. The least I can do is to be faithful to him.* This thought reminds me and motivates me to be holy.

The second thing that motivates me personally to live a holy life is the promise of future blessings. So many times in the Bible, God promises both immediate and future rewards to those who choose to be holy, including the promise from Psalm 1 noted earlier in this chapter. Another example of a promise that has helped me in the area of purity is Matthew 5:8, where Jesus said, "Blessed are the pure in heart, for they shall see God." I want to experience God in my everyday life, and yet it's obvious from this verse that I will not see Jesus in my daily life if I'm not pure. God also promises rewards in heaven for those who live holy lives. He wouldn't promise these future blessings if it weren't possible for us to be holy.

Now before I move to my final thoughts in this chapter, I want to spend a little extra time talking about the sexual purity mentioned above. You see, sexual purity and personal holiness go hand in hand, and experiencing sexual purity is the greatest challenge many young people face today. Well, all people, not just young people.

Taking Down the High Places

Recently I've been studying the book of 2 Kings, a book that's helped me to fall more in love with God because it shows how much God loves the world and is faithful to keep his promises.

Long after King David of Israel died, his son, Solomon, was king of Israel. Israel struggled with worshipping foreign gods for hundreds of years until they were taken into captivity by Assyria as a result of this sin. Solomon had many wives, married many foreign women, and built altars on high places and elevated sites on top of the mountain so his foreign wives could worship their false pagan god, Baal.

Over the years, some good kings of Judah removed Baal worship in Jerusalem, but they didn't remove the high places. Therefore, the temptation to worship Baal, the god of fertility whose worship was sexual in nature, remained. It wouldn't take long for Israel to fall into full-blown apostasy (the rejection of God) because of these high places. We see one of these instances of a good king removing Baal worship in the city but failing to remove the high places in 2 Kings 12:2–3: "Jehoash did what was right in the eyes of the LORD all his days, because Jehoiada the priest instructed him. Nevertheless, the high places were not taken away; the people continued to sacrifice and make offerings on the high places."

The high places were so entrenched in their culture; they seemed so normal that even the good kings did not think to remove them. What are the high places in your life? In other words, what are your blind spots or the areas of sin that you've gotten so accustomed to that you not only can't seem to stop doing them, but they seem normal?

In today's culture, sexual immorality is one of our high places. Kevin DeYoung says,

> If we could transport Christians from almost any other
> century to any of today's Christian countries in the West,
> I believe what would surprise them most is how at home
> Christians are with sexual impurity. It doesn't shock
> us. It doesn't upset us. It doesn't offend our consciences.
> In fact, unless it's really destructive, sexual impurity
> seems normal, just a way of life, and often downright
> entertaining.[3]

In our culture, nothing is more essential to our identity as human beings than the freedom to express ourselves sexually and use our bodies as we choose. But God says the body belongs to him, not to us. When we gave our lives to Christ, we gave him everything:

our time, our careers, our finances, our hopes and dreams, and yes, even our bodies. "Or do you not know that your body is a temple of the Holy Spirit within you, whom you have from God? You are not your own, for you were bought with a price. So glorify God in your body" (1 Cor. 6:19–20).

How are you doing in the area of sexual purity? If you are like most "normal people," you are having a difficult time. I don't want to trivialize this area or make it sound like it's easily solved. However, I do want you to take heart and know that with Christ all things are possible.

It might require hard work and due diligence, but with God's help you can conquer this area of your life. The Bible is clear that it is possible to live sexually pure lives.

We just need to believe in our hearts that it's possible and allow the Holy Spirit to change us through God's Word. Remember, it is God's will that you experience sexual purity, and he will provide all the help you need in this area or any other area.

If you've been broken in the area of sexual purity, I'd also encourage you to open up to someone about your struggle to live a sexually pure life. God knew it would be impossible for us to live holy lives alone; so he gave us both his Spirit and the church to encourage us. You don't have to open up to everyone and air out all your specific dirty laundry, but it's important to be open to someone who really loves Jesus so they can encourage you and help you to navigate through your trials.

If you need help with an addiction to Internet pornography, I'd strongly encourage you to go to CovenantEyes.com to purchase their software for your phone and computer to help with accountability. If you don't have money to pay for software right now, xxxchurch.com offers the best free accountability software. The important thing is that you find at least one or two people to whom you can confide about your brokenness in the area of sexual purity.

If sexual immorality is not one of your high places, you may have another high place or area of constant struggle. Regardless of the sin, these high places will keep you from experiencing God and having intimacy with him. The last area I want to discuss in this chapter is our thinking. Not only does God require us to live holy lives externally, but he wants holiness to be reflected in our thinking as well.

Thinking the Way God Wants Us to Think

One of the most powerful ways that we can worship God and glorify him is through our thinking. Recently God has been teaching me that when we think the way he wants us to think, it improves our overall emotional well-being.

Emotional well-being is a term that has seen increasing use in recent decades. The implications of decreased emotional well-being are related to mental health concerns such as stress, depression, and anxiety. These in turn can contribute to physical illnesses such as digestive disorders, sleep disturbances, and general lack of energy.

On the positive side, enhanced emotional well-being is seen to contribute to increased coping ability, self-esteem, performance and productivity at work, and even longevity.

In Philippians 4:8, Paul said, "Finally, brothers, whatever is true, whatever is honorable, whatever is just, whatever is pure, whatever is lovely, whatever is commendable, if there is any excellence, if there is anything worthy of praise, think about these things." This is God's command for us to think about things that please the Lord.

And it's not just the Bible that encourages us to think positively. Many studies have been done on the human brain and how it reacts to positive and negative emotions. Studies such as those conducted by the psychology departments at the University of Michigan and

Florida State University[4] have shown that positive emotions trigger upward spirals toward emotional well-being.

These studies have shown that pleasant emotions such as joy, thankfulness, and love actually increase brain dopamine or neurotransmitters that cause us to have emotional well-being.[5] In short, thinking about positive things causes us to have positive emotional well-being, while negative emotions such as cynicism, anger, or being judgmental toward someone can cause us to have a poor emotional well-being.

Sophia Array is a student at the University of Miami. I met her recently while on a mission trip in Brooklyn, New York. Last year, as a junior, she became a follower of Christ when she placed her faith in Jesus.

I asked Sophia to share what she has learned about surrendering her life fully to Jesus, and this is what she said:

> From a very early age I was picked on at school and
> made fun of by my peers. Without even realizing it, I
> allowed their rejection to define me. I believed the hurt-
> ful things they said about me and felt like I was worth-
> less. I coped with the despair and self-hate by shoving
> the pain into the deepest parts of me and making sure
> they were never exposed. For twenty years I carried
> this anguish inside. I felt hopeless because my accom-
> plishments and success did not skim the surface of my
> despair.
>
> In my third year of college, I met Jesus and I sur-
> rendered my life to him, but with limitations. I would
> follow God and put my faith in Jesus, but I did not
> believe God could love me because I could not love
> myself. But God still showered my life with grace and
> gently unraveled the pain I had so tightly packaged. He

also placed people in my life who loved and guided me out of my hopelessness.

I could not live a surrendered life until I accepted that Jesus loved me. He exposed the lies that made me believe I would never be worth anything, and he healed my heart and soul with his love. Since I placed my trust in God, he has released the choking grasp that my self-hate had. I now wake up every day and give God control of my life because he healed my brokenness and began weaving it into his story of redemption.

Sophia's story demonstrates that it's a struggle to be perfect in your devotion to God, and God knows this and knows our hearts. God also knows that when we are willing to do what he wants us to do and to think the way he wants us to think, our love toward him will slowly but surely continue to grow.

If I think about how much I've grown in the past month, I may not see much growth. However, if I think about how much more devoted to God I am now than I was twenty years ago, it's encouraging. I'm much more devoted and in love with God than I was then.

Your devotion to God *will* continue to grow if you continue to take even small steps of faith each day. While reading this book, you've probably identified a lot of different growth steps you can take, but don't worry about doing everything at once. After you finish this book, determine just two or three steps you'll adopt to get closer to God. Then in six months or a year, I encourage you to go through the book again to discover a couple more growth steps to take. Growing in devotion is a life-long process.

Notes

[1] C. S. Lewis, *Reflections on the Psalms* (New York: Harcourt Brace Jovanovich, 1958), 62.

[2] Kevin DeYoung, *The Hole in Our Holiness: Filling the Gap between Gospel Passion and the Pursuit of Godliness* (Wheaton: Crossway Books, 2012), Kindle edition.

[3] Ibid.

[4] Barbara Frederickson and Thomas Joiner, "Positive Emotions Trigger Upward Spirals toward Emotional Well-Being," *Psychological Science* 13 (2002), 172–75, accessed January 19, 2015, http://www.ecu.edu/cs-cas/psyc/upload /Fredrickson-Joiner-2002.pdf.

[5] F. G. Ashby, A. M. Isen, and A. U. Turken, "A Neuropsychological Theory of Positive Affect and Its Influence on Cognition," *Psychological Review* 106 (1999), 529–50, accessed January 19, 2015, http://rlrw.bnu.edu.cn/NewsImage /2012513225934.pdf.

CHAPTER
~7~

> # I Will Say What
> # You Want Me to Say

Few things are worse than finding a tick on one's
private parts.

Three years ago, my wife Elizabeth was driving on a busy highway when she heard our son Clark, who was seven at the time,
shriek, "What is that?" He then started screaming frantically, "Get it
off! Get it off! What is it?? Look, Wyatt! What do you think that is?"

Wyatt, his older brother, said, "What? Let me see . . . oh, no,
Clark! Does that have six legs or eight legs? If it has eight legs, it
could be . . . yep, it's a brown recluse spider. I'm sorry, Clark. Brown
recluses are one of the most deadly spiders there are, you know."

Let me go back to my first statement above. Few things are
worse than finding a tick on one's private area, except for when
someone tells you it's a brown recluse spider!

The yelling, shrieking, and total hysteria that ensued were deafening and nearly caused Elizabeth to get into an accident. As quickly as she could, she pulled the van over and climbed to the backseat. After examining the bug on Clark, she said as soothingly as she could, "Clark, it's okay. It's only a tick. You're going to live."

Clark's screams ensued as Elizabeth attempted to remove the tick, but it wasn't budging. Afraid of causing an infection or too much pain for Clark, she drove her screaming patient to a nearby Urgent Care Center. As Elizabeth and the kids entered the doctor's office, everyone in the waiting room as well as every nurse behind the desk knew they had an urgent situation. Clark was inconsolable. The nurse's eyes grew wide when Elizabeth whispered the reason for their visit.

Immediately, Elizabeth, Clark, and our three other children were ushered back to an examining room, and a doctor rushed in. Clark's shrieking continued. When the doctor saw the tick and its unhappy victim, his eyes widened, and he quickly left to recruit more help.

Wyatt, who was still going on about brown recluse spiders, was sent out of the examining room, but he continued to ask questions through the closed door. He wasn't helping. All the male doctors and nurses were very empathetic toward Clark. Two male doctors poked their heads into the room to offer suggestions for various numbing agents. All of them were feeling his pain.

It took two doctors, a nurse, and more than half an hour of prying and poking to finally get the tick off poor Clark. Elizabeth held down Clark, giving constant reassurance and pausing every few minutes to say to Clark's older brother, "Wyatt, stay out . . . no, it's not off yet. You are not helping!" By the time they were finished, Elizabeth and Clark had to go home and crash to get over the emotional meltdown of the day.

We often laugh now when we retell the story of Clark's traumatic experience and how Wyatt poured gasoline on the fire with his words. To Clark at the time, however, Wyatt's words were more than upsetting.

He could have offered words of comfort or hope, but, of course, a ten-year-old didn't think to comfort his ailing brother.

Sometimes we can be like Wyatt when others are discouraged or are hurting. God cares about the down and out, the discouraged and the broken. When we say things that cause others to get discouraged or to lose hope, we're not in tune with the heart of God. In a way, we're saying that God isn't in control of our lives or the world around us.

Two kinds of people don't show God they love him by the way they speak, and both can be found in Jesus' parable of the lost sons.

A good friend of mine who is a Bible teacher, Jim Hardin, refers to the first kind of person as the "accidental Pharisee." We discussed who Pharisees were in Jesus' day back in Chapter Two. In case you've forgotten, they were religious leaders who followed the rules in the Bible but didn't actually love God. They looked like good people on the outside, but their hearts were in the wrong place.

The Accidental Pharisee

Are you quick to break relationships with those who don't believe the same as you? Perhaps you engage in conversations where you tend to evaluate others' actions or beliefs. Are you at odds with others' decisions without taking time to pray about their decisions? Do you use social media to criticize or evaluate others?

If you do any of these things, you just might be an accidental Pharisee. I will confess I am a recovering accidental Pharisee. At times, I've answered yes to every one of the questions listed above. That's why, unfortunately, the story of the older son in Luke 15 hits so close to home for me.

Accidental Pharisees start with the best intentions. They study the Bible, try to understand God's rules, and they do their best to follow them. Of course, even the best Pharisee can't follow every rule in the Bible. So on top of being judgmental, they're also hypocritical.

A few years ago, I experienced conflict with another guy. I'll call him Doug.

I was talking negatively about Doug one day to another Christian friend when he said, "Chad, I've noticed recently that you've complained a lot about Doug lately, but I haven't heard you say anything nice about him. Doug's got some issues for sure, but you know he's got some good qualities about him as well. He's not all bad."

I was immediately convicted by my friend's words and responded, "I'm sorry about that. You're right. Doug does have a lot of good qualities, but I've been focusing on the bad ones. Will you forgive me for what I've said? I promise you I'll do a better job of focusing on the good things about him. I commit to you that I'll do better, and I want you to call me out if I say anything negative."

Do you know what happened when I stopped talking negatively about Doug and started thinking the best about him? The conflict stopped. I sat down with him one day and confessed to him that I had not been thinking the best about him, and he confessed he hadn't been thinking the best of me either.

We became much better friends that day, and three years later we're close friends. Had I not confessed my sin to him and started speaking well of him, I would have missed out on a very dear relationship.

A key passage regarding the accidental Pharisee is found in Matthew 23:

> Then Jesus said to the crowds and to his disciples, "The scribes and the Pharisees sit on Moses' seat, so do and observe whatever they tell you, but not the works they do. For they preach, but do not practice. They tie up

heavy burdens, hard to bear, and lay them on people's shoulders, but they themselves are not willing to move them with their finger." (vv. 1–4)

The reason Jesus got especially angry with the Pharisees is because their message was the opposite of God's message. Jesus was sharing the good news that even though we could never measure up to God's standard of perfection, he still made a way for us to be with him by sending Jesus to die for us.

God showed us his unmerited favor through Christ, and the gospel is a message that we can be free from the burden of our sin. Yet the Pharisees were adding to the people's burden instead of helping them to take the burden away.

When we are judgmental toward someone in a hypocritical way like the Pharisees, we are only adding to their burden instead of helping them to find freedom in the gospel. You may think, "Well so-and-so is a Christian, and they should know better." But being devoted to God means that we correct someone who is in error in a loving way. We don't talk about them behind their backs.

Just because someone is a follower of Christ doesn't mean they're a mature follower of Christ. In order to become more mature in their faith, they need to understand the gospel better so they can experience God's amazing grace even more.

Instead of producing more Christ followers, accidental Pharisees reproduce more Pharisees. Instead of cheering others on in their walks of faith, they critique (and I don't mean constructive criticism). They take the role of being the judge from God, who is the only one qualified to be The Judge. "There is only one lawgiver and judge, he who is able to save and to destroy. But who are you to judge your neighbor?" (Jas. 4:12).

So how do we get rid of the part of us that's a Pharisee?

First, attempt to starve it. I've found that if I avoid conversations where someone is judging someone else, my tendency to judge will not be fed and become active. I've also learned to constantly look closely at my own sinful heart and remember the gospel.

This is why it's so important to study God's word and to practice hearing the music of the gospel as we discussed in Chapter Four. Countless times I've been unfaithful to God, and yet he remains faithful to me. How can I possibly judge others when I've been just as unfaithful as they have?

No one aspires to be a Pharisee.

We set out with the best intentions, but our self-righteousness and tendency to judge can quickly derail our attempts to be as encouraging as Christ. Equally as dangerous is another type of attitude that doesn't show God's love, and it's also rooted in our tendency to judge and in our self-righteousness. It's known as the cynical spirit.

The Cynic

Are you cynical? Do you bad-mouth government leaders God has placed in your life without praying for them regularly? Maybe you avoid politics but find it easy to be critical of your teachers, parents, or boss. Would others describe you as a "glass half empty" person who usually sees the worst in or thinks the worst about other people? If so, you just might be cynical in spirit.

I have come to learn that one of my faults is that I can become overly cynical when I'm around others who talk critically. Instead of trying to offer hope, I'm tempted to join right in and become more cynical. Even worse, sometimes I instigate conversations like this.

Before I entered full-time ministry, I held a position as a supervisor in a paper mill. Most days I joined my coworkers at lunch. One of them passionately loved listening to a famous radio show led by a celebrity who bad-mouthed the government and the direction of our country. By the end of our lunch outing, I felt bitter toward the government and discouraged that our country was falling to pieces.

Have you watched the news lately? Doesn't it seem that 99 percent of what's reported is bad news? I'm convinced that there are great things happening all over the country, but news stations must get better ratings when bad news is reported. Negative news connects with those who struggle with fear. We must not hold on to fear, however. There is hope.

The message of good news in the Bible can replace our fear if we study the Bible daily. God is in control. He knows about all the brokenness, pain, and suffering in the world. That's why he sent Jesus to rescue the world and to eventually put things back in order. God had and still has a plan.

When we say discouraging words or keep a cynical attitude, we forget that God is in control. What's worse, when we make cynical comments about our leaders, the government, parents, teachers, or bosses, we're actually saying that God is not in control. Our words enable fear to get the best of us.

The prophet Isaiah lived during one of the most evil times in ancient Israelite history. He warned God's people that Israel would be destroyed if they continued to worship idols instead of following God, but he also communicated hope when he said in 9:6–7:

> For to us a child is born, to us a son is given; and the
> government shall be upon his shoulder, and his name
> shall be called Wonderful Counselor, Mighty God,
> Everlasting Father, Prince of Peace. Of the increase of
> his government and of peace there will be no end, on
> the throne of David and over his kingdom, to establish
> it and to uphold it with justice and righteousness from
> this time forth and forevermore.

Jesus, his disciples, and the apostle Paul all lived during the reign of the Roman Empire, one of the most evil empires in history. Sex slavery, murder, and other heinous crimes (which we still see around the world today) were prominent; still, Paul told the church in Rome, "We know that for those who love God all things work together for good, for those who are called according to his purpose" (Rom. 8:28).

Time and time again during times of suffering, God communicates hope throughout the Bible, and we must learn not only to communicate this hope, but to believe it as well.

Thankfully, I've been convicted of my cynicism, primarily through studying the Bible. The key passage God has used to help me overcome my cynicism is Colossians 3:15–17. I refer to this passage as the Thankfulness Commandments, and it has literally helped to transform me into a much more positive person.

The Thankfulness Commandments

In Colossians 3:15–17, Paul writes,

> Let the peace of Christ rule in your hearts, to which
> indeed you were called in one body. And be thankful.
> Let the word of Christ dwell in you richly, teaching and
> admonishing one another in all wisdom, singing psalms
> and hymns and spiritual songs, with thankfulness in
> your hearts to God. And whatever you do, in word
> or deed, do everything in the name of the Lord Jesus,
> giving thanks to God the Father through him.

One could paraphrase those three verses above by just giving the command: Be thankful. Be thankful. Be thankful.

About fourteen months ago, my seven-year-old, Evelyn, was diagnosed with an eye condition called amblyopia. It had gone undiagnosed for six years, causing blindness in her right eye. Her brain and eye weren't working together properly. In order to regain sight, Evelyn began wearing a patch over her good eye to force her brain to begin using her bad eye.

At first, she ran into walls and couldn't see anything. Then, the patching seemed to help Evelyn tremendously. Within the first couple of weeks, she went from being nearly completely blind to being able to get around and function fairly well with just her bad eye. After a few months, though, her progress slowed down.

Fourteen months later, Evelyn still wears a patch over one eye for at least several hours a day. She's been a trooper. After having to explain a hundred times to kids at school and in our community why she wears a patch, she has stayed positive. Every month she enters her eye doctor appointment desperately hoping to be done wearing a patch, and although she has been disappointed time and time again by the words "keep patching," she has maintained a good attitude.

Sometimes my attitude hasn't been nearly as good as Evelyn's. We were shocked to discover her blindness in that eye during an annual wellness check. How had we missed it for six years? If we had caught it earlier, could we have prevented permanent loss of sight? The doctor told us that the earlier you catch amblyopia, the greater the chance of complete recovery.

Every time I've started to get discouraged about Evelyn's condition, the thankfulness commands are what have helped to keep me grounded. Do you remember the story I shared of the attack of the poisonous caterpillar? After Elizabeth was stung by that poisonous caterpillar while pregnant with Clark, her body never seemed to fully recover. Pre-term labor contractions were a constant problem during her pregnancies with both Clark and Evelyn. In fact, if it weren't for modern medicine, she never would have been able to carry Evelyn to full term.

When I think about the miracle of Evelyn's birth, it reminds me to be thankful that she is here. God allowed us to have her. This thankfulness overcomes my discouragement from any trials we're currently facing regarding her eyesight.

In what ways has having a thankful heart helped you? Can you begin to apply the thankfulness commands to your life so that you can overcome discouragement and cynicism? Be thankful. Be thankful. Be thankful.

Being thankful and rejecting judgment and cynicism have transformed my heart, yet Matthew 18 has made the biggest difference in my life in helping me to "say what you want me to say."

The Matthew 18 Principle

Many years ago, while on a summer mission trip in Daytona Beach, Florida, a mentor of mine, Earle Chute, shared three Bible verses to help me deal with a conflict between a couple of guys in my Bible study. The verses were Matthew 18:15–17.

> If your brother sins against you, go and tell him his fault,
> between you and him alone. If he listens to you, you
> have gained your brother. But if he does not listen, take
> one or two others along with you, that every charge may
> be established by the evidence of two or three witnesses.
> If he refuses to listen to them, tell it to the church. And
> if he refuses to listen even to the church, let him be to
> you as a Gentile and a tax collector.

I followed the instructions in these three verses and taught others to follow them that summer. It was amazing how effective these verses were in helping navigate through conflict. After that summer, I've taught the principles I learned to hundreds of college students and young adults. "The Matthew 18 Principle" outlines Jesus' three-step process for conflict resolution.

Jesus knew his followers. He knew they would have conflict with one another. No one is perfect. We all make mistakes by doing and saying what we don't want or mean to do. We inadvertently hurt others by our comments and actions.

There are many topics Jesus didn't directly address in his teaching. He never addressed smoking cigars or nose piercings. He wasn't specific in how many times a day we should pray or exactly how much money we should give to the poor. He was, however, quite clear about how he wanted us to deal with conflict when it inevitably came. Talking behind each other's backs and bottling our emotions weren't part of his plan. He simply wanted us to open up and share our hurts or frustrations with those who have hurt us.

Aaron Tripp embraced the Matthew 18 Principle.

I met Aaron during his first day on campus as a freshman at the College of Charleston, and nearly five years later I was honored to stand as a groomsman in his wedding. God transformed Aaron from a new Christian struggling to find identity and joy to a man who was fully devoted to God. I had the privilege of watching the change occur firsthand. Here are Aaron's words on how the Matthew 18 Principle helped him have more genuine relationships:

> Many people do not like to be labeled with stereotypes, but I look back at my first few years in college and realize that I was a stereotypical male. I kept all of my emotions to myself and never let anyone know that I cared. Applying the Matthew 18 Principle helped me to break out of my emotionally void pattern of relationships.
>
> Daniel, a classmate at the College of Charleston, and I didn't like each other. We were usually overly sarcastic and dismissive when we were together at Cru events. I saw him as a Goody-Two-shoes, and I'm fairly certain he thought I was a delinquent. That all changed on a mission trip to New York City my junior year. Daniel was giving me "the stink eye" for two or three days, every time I gave instructions to the younger students, including Daniel. I decided that rather than let this

tension continue, I should reach out to him and see if I had done anything to hurt him.

I waited until we were alone, and I asked him why he had been eyeballing me for the past few days. Had I done anything to hurt his feelings? Daniel laughed and told me that the opposite was true. He had come to respect me over the past few days; the staring was due to shock. He thought I disliked him, just as I thought he disliked me. So for the past few days, we had been continuing a pattern of discord, when really we both had grown to respect each other.

I do not know what would have happened if I hadn't approached Daniel that day, but I do know that we grew to be very close friends. Daniel and I taught a Bible study together the following year and prayed regularly together and for one another.

Notice that Aaron was tempted to say nothing to Daniel regarding the tension he sensed between them. We've all experienced that temptation. It's easier to not say anything and pretend there's not a real problem in our relationships, hoping that tension will just go away on its own in time.

Aaron rejected the temptation and talked to Daniel (following the first step in the Matthew 18 Principle) because Jesus commanded him to do so. God desired both Aaron and Daniel not only to get along but also to grow in their intimacy with him. By saying to Daniel what God wanted Aaron to say, Aaron was showing love and obedience to God.

What opportunities do you have to show God you love him by saying what he wants you to say? Take time to evaluate and think if you are in conflict with someone. Who can you give words of encouragement or hope to today? Words are so powerful.

Remember that when we give our lives to God, our lives aren't just about us anymore. Our lives are about him. When we make an effort to show him we love him, he will allow us to experience greater joy than we can ever imagine.

Think of it this way: Have you ever heard of Gary Chapman's book, *The Five Love Languages*? Chapman explains that there are five ways we can show love toward and receive love from other people: words of affirmation, acts of service, giving/receiving gifts, spending quality time, and physical touch.[1]

God also has love languages, very similar ones. Instead of sharing words of affirmation, we can show God love by saying what he wants us to say, affirming both God and others around us. Doing what he wants us to do is the equivalent of Chapman's acts of service, the kind ways we help and serve those we love. Since we can't see or touch God, showing love through physical touch doesn't apply, but we can give him quality time. As we have already seen, quality time involves both studying his Word and going where he wants us to go. Finally, we can show God love by giving him gifts, much as we give our loved ones gifts. In the next chapter, we'll explore how God is glorified when we give back to him.

Note

[1]Gary Chapman, *The Five Love Languages: The Secret to Love That Lasts* (Chicago: Moody Publishers, 2010), Kindle edition.

CHAPTER
~8~

I Will Give What You Want Me to Give

I'll never forget my first week of being a father. That was fourteen years ago. When Elizabeth went into labor with our son Wyatt, I nervously proclaimed to Elizabeth on the way to the hospital, "I'm not ready for this! Are you sure you're going to have this baby tonight? I don't think I'm prepared to be a father." Elizabeth just looked at me in disbelief, and said, "Umm . . . ready or not, he's coming."

Sure enough, Wyatt soon arrived. He was a beautiful 7 lb. 4 oz. baby boy, and I loved him as soon as I saw him. I still felt scared, but the instant love I felt for him was powerful. When we brought Wyatt home from the hospital a few days later, I was on pins and needles. Wyatt had acid reflux and woke up once or twice each night choking on what he spit up. Twice he stopped breathing and turned blue. Afraid that we would have another scare, I constantly watched him to make sure his chest was moving as he slept.

One night that first week, Elizabeth and I were in our living room having a conversation. I sat on the couch with my legs perched up on the coffee table. My knees were bent with Wyatt balanced in the middle of my legs. He just lay there looking up, watching me. Elizabeth walked into the other room to get something to drink.

Suddenly, right in the middle of our conversation, I sensed in the pit of my stomach that something wasn't right. I looked down at Wyatt and watched his chest to make sure he was breathing, but I couldn't see it moving. I put my finger below his nose to see if I could feel his breath, but I couldn't feel anything. Staring at the ceiling with his eyes open, he had this glazed look on his face. I moved my hands over his eyes to try to get him to blink, but his eyes didn't move. He just continued to stare at the ceiling. That's when I completely lost control of my emotions.

I immediately went into hysterics and shouted, "Call 911! Wyatt's not breathing! He's dead! He's dead!"

Elizabeth sprinted to the phone and called an ambulance. I could hear her panicked voice as she relayed our address to the dispatcher. I continued to shout, "He's dead! He's not breathing!"

Right as Elizabeth hung up, Wyatt must have noticed his daddy going into hysterics. He turned his eyes from the ceiling toward me and started moving his hands as if he was waving at me. He wasn't dead, and he hadn't stopped breathing, at least not for more than a few seconds. He was just fine.

I then regained control of my emotions and said with a nonchalant tone, "Oh, never mind. He's breathing, Elizabeth. False alarm."

Elizabeth replied, "What do you mean he's fine? Well, I just called 911!"

"You called 911?"

"Yes," Elizabeth responded firmly, "You said our newborn wasn't breathing and to call, so I called 911."

"Well, now what are we going to do? Doesn't it cost money to have an ambulance come to your house? How are we going to explain that the baby's fine?"

Less than a minute later, a fire truck and an ambulance pulled up in front of our house. The fire station was located literally right outside our little subdivision. I could see a first responder running up our front steps.

As we opened the door, I looked at Elizabeth and said to the paramedic, "I . . . uh, well, I think he's okay now, but we had a scare with our baby."

The paramedic took Wyatt out of my arms and replied, "The dispatcher said your baby stopped breathing. Let me take a look at him."

Trying to help me out, Elizabeth said, "He's breathing now. We think he's going to be okay."

"His color looks excellent," he said as he took a look at Wyatt's eyes and peered into his mouth. He then shot me a quizzical look and asked, "Are you guys first-time parents?"

This embarrassing-but-true story reminds me that perception doesn't always match up with reality. In that one scary moment, it appeared to me that Wyatt had stopped breathing. Obviously, that wasn't the case. Wyatt was fine, but the illusion that he was dead caused both Elizabeth and me to make an irrational decision and erroneously call 911.

The illusion that we are in control often leads us to make poor decisions regarding where we go and how we spend our time. It also affects whether or not we will be obedient to God and how we communicate with both God and others. But in reality, we're not in control and never will be.

That's probably a good thing. We're self-centered and often make mistakes. Fortunately for us, God *is* in control, and he's a good God who never makes mistakes.

One example is the area of personal finances. Most people prefer to call the shots and completely control their finances without regard to what God's Word instructs. Many learn the hard way, and a few never learn or experience the blessings of following the truth that all of our money and possessions belong to God. As we've discussed before, when we surrender our lives to God, *everything* belongs to him.

Some followers of Christ believe the misconception that God only wants a certain percentage of our income as our "tithes and offerings." That line of thinking may lead us to believe that after we give the first tenth of our income, the rest is ours to spend as we see fit.

The problem is that the Bible never says that anything belongs to us. In fact, it says the opposite: that everything belongs to God. I love how Eugene Peterson's *The Message* phrases Psalm 24:1: "God claims Earth and everything in it. God claims World and all who live on it."

When we live with the mind-set that everything we have belongs to God, it leads us to be ready and willing to give anything we have, even the shirts off our backs, when God makes it clear that he wants us to give.

Always Be Prepared to Give What God Wants

On a recent Friday night at 11:30, I received a call from Elizabeth that was disheartening. She calmly said, "Well, it hasn't been a good night for my minivan."

Elizabeth had just spent five hours at a friend's house getting our daughter Josilynn's hair braided. As I mentioned before, Josilynn is biracial. It's been amazing having her as a daughter. Her adoption has broken down racial barriers for our family, and we've gained friends that we might never have known.

One of those new friendships is with an African American family we met at football games. Our son Wyatt is one of the few Caucasian boys on his seventh-grade football team. Elizabeth first met Kayla and her husband, John, at one of Wyatt's practices, and Josilynn immediately became best friends with their daughter Reagan.

After the first couple of practices, Josilynn came home and proudly announced, "Reagan's my best friend. She has brown skin like me. Clark, Wyatt, and Evelyn have yellow skin like Mommy, but Reagan looks like me. When can I play with my friend who looks like me again?"

Elizabeth made a point to get to know this family better, and she quickly hit it off with Kayla. They've been friends ever since. A few weeks ago, Kayla offered to braid Josilynn's hair and show Elizabeth how to do it. Elizabeth was thrilled by the offer and scheduled a time the following Friday evening.

During the first few hours of the long braiding process, Kayla and Elizabeth began discussing their spiritual journeys. Kayla had grown up going to church, but she stopped going because many of her friends who said they were Christians were living hypocritical lifestyles.

Kayla hadn't been to church since she was a child, with the exception of major holidays or for weddings. She also talked about their family's financial struggles. Their landlord had just increased their rent by fifty dollars, and Kayla didn't know how they were going to afford the extra burden.

When Kayla was close to finishing Josilynn's hair, her husband, John, left to pick up some dinner. When he returned, he walked in with a defeated look on his face. He said to Elizabeth, "I just hit your minivan with my car. I saw it and was trying to be extra careful not to hit it, but our driveway was pitch black. I am so sorry, but I scraped the side of your car."

During the last half hour of Josilynn's braiding, Elizabeth endured awkward silence. She could tell there was tension between John and Kayla, even though Kayla didn't say much. It was especially awkward because Kayla had just shared their financial struggles, and both John and Kayla just looked sick at their stomachs. As Elizabeth was leaving, John told her he would text the information to her about his car insurance.

After Elizabeth called on her way home to tell me that her minivan had been damaged and to describe the financial plight Kayla and John were in, I prayed and asked the Lord what to do. We'd had accidents before, but I can't remember ever seeking God's direction on what to do about an insurance claim. This time it felt different, and I felt the urge to pray.

We were just getting to know John and Kayla. We knew they had strayed from the church, and I didn't want anything to come between us as we were just starting to build a friendship with them. I prayed, "What should we do?"

As I prayed and asked God for guidance, a thought popped into my head: *How much is the eternal life of a person worth?*

Elizabeth arrived home, and we both looked at her car under the spotlight in our driveway. It looked pretty bad. The shiny panel above her driver's side front wheel had been bent badly. When I opened her driver's side door, I heard a loud screeching metal-to-metal sound. Something was blocking its path, trying to prevent it from opening. We talked about it for a few minutes, and Elizabeth again shared the financial struggles of Kayla and John. She didn't think they were in a position to pay the deductible or afford the insurance increase that often accompanied a new claim.

The thought popped back into my head again: *How much is the eternal life of a person worth?* Suddenly the answer became clear. The life of one person is priceless. It's worth more than all the money in the world.

"Well," Elizabeth asked, "What are you thinking? What do you think we should do?"

I responded, "I think every time we open your car door, we should remember to pray for John and Kayla, and I think you should text him back and let him know it isn't so bad. We're not going to file an insurance claim."

Elizabeth texted John, and we continued to drive her minivan during the rest of the weekend. Every time one of us opened the door and heard the loud, obnoxious screeching sound, we stopped for a minute and prayed for them right there.

The next week, Elizabeth took Wyatt to his football practice while I took Clark and Evelyn to their soccer games. When John and Kayla saw Elizabeth, they walked over with smiling faces and sat down, giving her a warm greeting. Elizabeth could tell they were both relieved that we weren't filing an insurance claim.

As Elizabeth sat with them and watched Wyatt's practice, Kayla said, "You know what? I love your kids. I don't think I've ever met such a nice young man as Wyatt. He seems so polite and kind for a seventh grader. Josilynn is so happy and sweet as well. Your family's different than anyone else we know. I want my kids to grow up having friends like your kids."

When Elizabeth got home later that evening and told me how happy John and Kayla were and what Kayla said to her, I was so full of joy. I knew we had done what God wanted us to do, and there's nothing quite like the joy of knowing you've been obedient to God.

I honestly don't know what we'll do about Elizabeth's minivan. We still haven't gotten it fixed because we don't have the extra money right now to pay our deductible. It's not exactly a new car, though, so we may just live with the dents. Regardless, we remember to pray for John and Kayla every time we open the door and hear the screeching sound.

Now, would it have been wrong to ask John and Kayla's insurance company to pay for the damages John caused? No, it would have been ethical to expect them to pay for it. The accident was John's fault, and he had a legal responsibility to pay for the damages.

However, something else was going on behind the scene that we could only have been made aware of if we were in tune with God's will. We'd been praying for them, asking God to give us an opportunity to talk with them about spiritual things. When an opening came for Elizabeth to ask spiritual questions, Kayla did open up and also shared about their financial struggles. John and Kayla were in a serious bind financially. Elizabeth and I don't have a lot of disposable income, but we certainly were in a better spot to pay for the damages to our car than they were.

It was clear to us that God wanted us to forgive John and Kayla and show them grace, not holding them responsible for the damages to our car. Does that mean that we'll never hold anyone responsible if they hit our car and cause damage? Probably not. We'll have to figure that out on a case-by-case basis. This time we felt led to give John and Kayla a gift by forgiving their debt to us.

My friend Patrick Dickerson is one of the most generous people I know. He's a business owner who knows he wasn't called to go into full-time ministry but to provide financial support to those who are in ministry. I recently asked Patrick what God has been teaching him, and he responded by saying he's learning to show mercy toward others. He's learning to love his neighbors the way the Good Samaritan loved his neighbor.

Who's Your Neighbor?

In Luke 10, a lawyer asked Jesus what one must do to have eternal life. Jesus responded by asking him what he thought the Bible said about it, and the man responded:

"You shall love the Lord your God with all your heart and with all your soul and with all your strength and with all your mind, and your neighbor as yourself." And he said to him, "You have answered correctly; do this, and you will live."

But he, desiring to justify himself, said to Jesus, "And who is my neighbor?" Jesus replied, "A man was going down from Jerusalem to Jericho, and he fell among robbers, who stripped him and beat him and departed, leaving him half dead. Now by chance a priest was going down that road, and when he saw him he passed by on the other side. So likewise a Levite, when he came to the place and saw him, passed by on the other side.

"But a Samaritan, as he journeyed, came to where he was, and when he saw him, he had compassion. He went to him and bound up his wounds, pouring on oil and wine. Then he set him on his own animal and brought him to an inn and took care of him. And the next day he took out two denarii and gave them to the innkeeper, saying, 'Take care of him, and whatever more you spend, I will repay you when I come back.' Which of these three, do you think, proved to be a neighbor to the man who fell among the robbers?" He said, "The one who showed him mercy." And Jesus said to him, "You go, and do likewise." (vv. 27–37)

Here are Patrick's words that he shared regarding what God has taught him through this passage about giving:

Mercy is intentional. Lately I have been struck by God's mercy, his intentional display of love toward me personally. There is so much hurt in the world. We are but a point, click, and screen touch away from images, videos, and sounds that burden my heart. So preoccupied am I with my own world. There never seems to be enough time, money, space, or resources at my disposal to accomplish what I want. Surely someone else will tend to those in need. I am just too busy.

Six years ago . . . I thought I was making the best decision in moving my family to another part of the state. We found a nice home on a small lake. We knew that our "new" home was old and would need some work; this is part of what made it affordable. We would use some of the money from the sale of our former home to pay for the much-needed work on our current and "new" fixer-upper, or so we thought.

Three years ago . . . life's struggles seemed impossible. Profits were in decline at work, and I was then paying three mortgages. Our former home hadn't sold, resulting in us putting our investment/rental home on the sales market, and our "new" fixer-upper home was less comfortable. We simply didn't have any additional funding to do any repairs. In the midst of our financial struggles, we were tempted to cut back on our giving but sensed God leading us to continue giving generously toward helping others, and so we did. We had to make sacrifices.

Today . . . as always, the needs of my family have been met. God has been merciful to my family and me. I was never forced into purchasing a home or making other poor financial choices deserving of hardship and suffering. God has taught me the value of mercy and instructed me to "go and do likewise." With his help, I will give more mercy.

An interesting thing about the story of the Good Samaritan in Luke 10 is that he was an enemy of the Jews. The priest and Levite in Jesus' parable should have been the Jewish man's friends, but they didn't stop to help him. They left him to die. The Samaritan, the man's enemy, was the one who stopped to take care of him. He even gave financially so that the man could stay in an inn while he recovered.

It's clear in this passage that Jesus wasn't just saying the person who lives next to us is our neighbor. Our neighbor is anyone, even an enemy, who needs our help and mercy. And like Patrick said, the reason we should show mercy is because God has been so merciful to us. He's done so much for us that the least we can do is to show others mercy.

How are you doing in this area? Are you giving generously back to God, or do you feel God is telling you in this passage that you need to give more?

Spend some time in prayer, asking God what he wants you to give. Consider making the following pledge and then looking around, finding where God is at work, and getting in the middle of his work by giving your time, talents, and finances toward that cause.

The Surrender Pledge

One thing many followers of Christ have found helpful and inspiring is to make a pledge to surrender their hearts to God. Personally, a few years ago I made a pledge by typing the following on a piece of paper and then signing it: *Lord Jesus, I surrender to you, and in the power of the Holy Spirit, I will go where you want me to go, do what you want me to do, say what you want me to say, and give what you want me to give.*

You can also make this pledge online. I'd encourage you to join the tens of thousands of others who have made this pledge by visiting www.cru.org/pledge. There are great resources on that website to help you to grow spiritually after you take the surrender pledge.

Now, I'll be the first to tell you that just because I made that pledge to God one day, it didn't mean I was automatically surrendered to God the next. I've had to repeat that pledge many more times in my prayers.

Writing that pledge on a piece of paper and then signing it was helpful, though, because it gave me a starting point. It was very specific because it listed all four areas (going, doing, saying, and giving) in my life that I wanted to give to God.

Long before I made this pledge, I had often confessed sinful areas of my life to God, ways that I'd broken his heart. By confessing this ever-changing list, I tried to tell God that I wanted to give myself completely to him. However, this practice didn't lend itself to forming an identifiable picture in my mind. But naming these four specific areas in the above pledge made my commitment to the Lord more tangible and real to me. It was a clear picture that has helped many others and me.

No doubt, as you've read these last four chapters, you've identified at least two or three action steps you need to take in order to live a more surrendered life. I encourage you to offer the surrender pledge to God and begin to take those steps.

Again, don't get discouraged or overwhelmed if you have a whole lot of steps you need to take. Just take one step now, mark your calendar to evaluate where you are in six months, and then take another step or two. Growth can be a slow process, but you'll see great progress a few years from now if you keep taking small steps. If I look back just a week, I won't see much growth in my spiritual life. But when I look back a year or two, I can see that God has blessed me with much spiritual growth.

Why do we *want* to go, do, say, and give as God pleases?

It all goes back to the adoption we talked about in Chapter Two.

When someone asks me what it means to be a Christian, the first thing I tell them is that it means we're adopted into the family of God. "To all who did receive him, who believed in his name, he gave the right to become children of God" (John 1:12).

Adoption is one of the most common metaphors Jesus used in the Bible to describe Christian faith. Once we're adopted, we're in the family.

Recently Josilynn has figured out what it means to be adopted. It's amazing how quickly kids understand complex concepts like that. We thought we'd have to explain adoption to her when she went to kindergarten, but because she's biracial and has skin color that's so much darker than Elizabeth's, at three years old she began asking questions Elizabeth didn't expect to answer for years.

Recently Josilynn got into trouble for being mean to her older sister, and after she had a time-out, I talked to her to make sure she understood why she was in trouble and to see if she was sorry for her actions.

In the middle of our conversation, Josilynn asked, "Am I still going to be in the family?"

"Of course, Josilynn," I responded. "You're a part of our family. You'll always be a part of our family. Do you know what your last name is?"

She looked at me and said, "Josilynn Young."

"That's right!" I said. "And do you know what Daddy's last name is?" She looked confused, so I helped her out by saying, "Young. Daddy's last name is Young. And do you know Mommy's last name?"

"Young?"

"That's right, Josilynn!" I said. We then went through the last names of all of her siblings so that she understood everyone in our family had the same last name.

I then said, "Josilynn, Mommy and I will always love you. We love you when you're good. We love you when you're bad. We just plain love you. You belong in the Young family. You always will . . . You're a Young!"

That's the way adoption works, and the same can be said about our adoption into God's family. He loves us when we're good. He loves us when we're bad. He just plain loves us, and he'll never leave us. We belong in his family.

When I explain our adoption into God's family to young Christians or to people who don't consider themselves Christians, I often get the question, "Well, if God loves us no matter what we do, then why should I do what he wants? Why should I try to be obedient and follow his commands?"

I ask them, "Why should my daughter Josilynn be obedient to follow the rules of our family?"

The answer is pretty simple. Josilynn is now in the Young family, and her mom and I have set rules that people in the Young family live by. We don't steal. We don't cheat. We treat others with respect. We don't lie. In fact, there are a whole host of values we live by in the Young family.

We expect Josilynn to abide by our rules. We didn't set them to harm her. In fact, the opposite is true. We set these rules to protect Josilynn and to help her to grow to have a good work ethic, a healthy marriage one day—so that she will grow up to contribute to society in a positive way.

The same can be said about our position as members of God's family. He has rules that his family members abide by. He wants to protect us. He wants us to have healthy families, and he wants us to contribute positively to the lives of those around us. God loves those who are broken, hurting, and who are down and out. He wants his family members to take care of those around us, just like the Good Samaritan in Jesus' parable.

This is why we *want* to go, do, say, and give what God wants. He's our Father, and we live to please him and live as those who are in God's family are supposed to live. We love God with all of our souls, being devoted to him, because he was so gracious to adopt us into his family.

There's one more area in which we can love God: With our minds. God doesn't want us to have blind faith. He wants us to grow intellectually in our understanding of both him and his creation. When we develop our minds, we not only appreciate him more, but we also become more effective in helping others to love God.

Part 3

All Your Mind

"Life is one big road with lots of
signs. So when you're riding through
the ruts, don't complicate your
mind. Flee from hate, mischief, and
jealousy. Don't bury your thoughts;
put your vision to reality.
Wake up and live!"

—Bob Marley

CHAPTER
~9~

Beware of
Green Biscuits!

The summer when I was twenty-two, sausage biscuits nearly killed me.

A recent college graduate and engaged to Elizabeth, I prepared to enter graduate school at Georgia Tech. I needed experience as a process engineer, and I was thrilled to find work as an intern in a paper mill in Charleston. Not only would I gain experience, but Elizabeth lived in Charleston, too. It seemed like the perfect opportunity.

My future in-laws, Chuck and Mary Mena, knew I wanted to save my pennies for married life, so they helped find a reasonably priced place for me to live during the summer. Ms. Ethel, a kind elderly woman they knew, lived by herself. Needing someone to keep her company, she seemed elated to have a summer guest. Little did Chuck and Mary Mena know they were inadvertently putting their future son-in-law's life, well . . . at least his GI system, at risk.

Ms. Ethel loved to cook. Every morning she greeted me with a plate full of sausage biscuits. As I sat in the living room recliner eating biscuits, from her spot on the couch next to me she told stories from her childhood.

At first the stories were quite interesting. She grew up during the Great Depression, and life then really contrasted to the life I lived. I heard family stories about her siblings, as well as high school and college adventures.

Soon a few trends became evident. Every fourth day or so, Ms. Ethel would begin repeating the stories almost in chronological order from her childhood to adulthood. Secondly, she showed displeasure when I tried to exit the conversations, or the house, for that matter. Thirdly, Ms. Ethel always seemed to do all the talking. I rarely had a chance to comment or share experiences from my life.

My days became predictable. I got out of the shower, dressed, and walked into the living room. After the sausage biscuits greeted me each morning, Ms. Ethel picked up wherever the previous story had left off, and after thirty minutes, I searched for an opportunity to leave for work.

When it was time to leave, I tried to interrupt her: "Ms. Eth . . . I need to . . . I'm sorry, but I . . . thank you for breakf . . . okay, I've gotta . . . bye, bye, Ms. Eth . . ."

After twenty to thirty minutes of concerted effort to leave politely each morning, I tried standing or walking toward the door. She would look frustrated and sneer, "Go ahead and just leave! That's what everyone else does!"

My heart broke for Ms. Ethel. Her loneliness was evident. The entire day at work, I'd feel rotten for leaving this elderly woman alone.

Elizabeth shared my concern for Ms. Ethel. In the evenings, we'd sit and listen to her stories together. Other times we'd have dates planned out, but leaving her was difficult. She desperately tried her best to keep us in the house with her.

Halfway through the summer, I noticed my morning sausage biscuits were light green. I tried inquiring about their color, but it was impossible to insert my questions into the conversation. Green color and all (and they seemed to get greener every day), I continued to eat the sausage biscuits.

Late in the summer, it occurred to me that Ms. Ethel's green biscuits were making me sick. My stomach cramped and ached throughout the workday; sometimes I even felt feverish. My gastrointestinal system was in turmoil.

Then one afternoon when I arrived back from work, an ambulance and police car occupied the driveway of Ms. Ethel's house. Ms. Ethel's son explained that she had become very ill, and it might be in my best interest to move out of the house.

Sadly, a few days later, Ms. Ethel passed away. After the funeral, Elizabeth's parents and I helped the family to clean her house.

We were all shocked to find dozens of green biscuits lining the shelves of the refrigerator. Apparently at the beginning of my stay, Ms. Ethel had bought enough biscuits to last for three months! The cause of my stomach ailments was confirmed.

The experience of living with Ms. Ethel was a challenging one. It recently occurred to me that many people probably feel frustrated with Christians in the same way. Christians often have interesting stories to tell about their faith journeys and about Christ, but they don't seem interested in listening to you. Their conversations are one-sided as they tell you how you should live your life.

Perhaps you grew up with parents who took you to church, but no one asked you about your doubts and struggles. Perhaps you were encouraged to have "blind faith" and accept teachings that didn't make sense to you. Perhaps you were afraid to even ask the questions your heart ached to know out of fear of looking stupid.

David Kinnaman describes today's teenagers and young adults like this: "A generation of young Christians believes that the churches in which they were raised were not safe and hospitable places to express doubts. Many feel that they have been offered slick or half-baked answers and 'talking points' they see among the older generations."[1]

Perhaps, like me, you've struggled to have faith.

A Younger Generation Struggling to Find Faith

During my freshman year in college, I nearly lost my Christian faith.

My dad pastored a church, so I always owned church clothes growing up. I rarely missed a Sunday service.

When I arrived at Clemson University as a student, however, my priorities changed. My parents lived two states away, and therefore, no one woke me on Sunday mornings to encourage me to go. I was used to having a community of friends, more like a family, at church. I attempted to fulfill that desire for community by pledging a fraternity. While I was immersed in a seemingly unending party scene, God seemed to be so far away, perhaps even nonexistent.

For nearly two weeks my first semester, I awoke each morning suffering from a hangover, not remembering the previous night's events. Disgusted and alarmed, over and over I declared that my drinking games were over, but each night my buddies coaxed me to a bar for yet another last beer.

During that period of binge drinking, a janitor violently awoke me one morning. He beat my head with a mop and yelled, "Get out of here right now! I'm calling the cops!"

Startled, I immediately ran toward an exit. I quickly recognized I was in a church sanctuary. In the hallway, a large mirror hung next to the exit. The reflection in the mirror brought me to a halt. Living in the fraternity, I had grown accustomed to seeing guys look pretty grizzly and hungover the morning after a party, but I barely recognized myself. I looked terrible.

Yet, I looked down and saw that I was wearing nice clothes. *A mysterious blue blazer and a tie?* I didn't know where the blue blazer came from, but the tie I recognized as the only one I brought to college. *What in the world? Where did this blazer come from? More importantly, what did I do last night?* I asked myself. I peeled off the blazer, dropped it, and ran out the building exit.

To this day, I've never figured out the story on that blazer. My freshman year clearly represented a very dark period of my life. As I reflect on my overnight stay on the church pew, I realize it revealed a truth about my life. Although I had put God on the back burner and was not living out my faith, in my heart I wanted to get things right with God. Even in my drunkenness, I desired to be near God.

If you happen to be a college student or if you've ever lived on a college campus, there's a good chance you can relate to my story in some way. Instead of the party scene, perhaps you've poured your life into your books or a dating relationship, and perhaps the busyness of life has gotten in the way of a genuine relationship with God.

One of the biggest barriers to a relationship with God is how we so easily become self-absorbed. Our lives slip into becoming mainly just about us, and we find our purpose and joy in things other than God. Research shows this is especially true when we're in college. According to a recent study by the Barna Group, 59 percent of the young people growing up in church are leaving the Christian faith in college.[2]

Recently, I walked the grounds at Kennesaw State University, enjoying a beautiful spring day. It marked my first visit to the Marietta campus of KSU, and the gorgeous scenery was a pleasant surprise. Home to roughly six thousand students, this campus is a tech school located just north of downtown Atlanta. I expected the campus to be dreary with plain brick buildings and parking lots, but blooming pink and red azaleas highlighted beautiful landscaping.

With permission from the administration, a few other campus ministers and I set up a booth to meet students in front of the student center. We simply wanted to see if enough students were interested in starting a new college ministry on campus. One student, a sophomore I'll call Brian, approached and asked about our new student group. I explained to him that we hoped to start a Christian group, and a guilty look came over his face.

"Well, I brought my Bible to college," Brian said, "but I haven't read it or gone to church."

I tried to help ease Brian's obvious feelings of guilt by saying, "That's okay. Neither did I when I was in college." I then told Brian my story (including the blue blazer experience), and he immediately relaxed. I asked him why he hasn't been to church in college.

"Mainly because I'm so busy," Brian said. Then he added, "Well, it's not just that I'm busy. I'm also having a lot of fun, and I'm afraid that if I go to church, I'll have to quit some of my fun activities."

I smiled reassuringly and responded, "Hey, why don't you get connected with our college group? I promise I won't make you quit any of your fun activities. I really think you could find some genuine friends in our group."

Brian agreed and shared his cell number. He seemed to appreciate my lack of judgment toward him. Later that day, Brian showed up at our very first group meeting on this new campus.

Brian's story almost seems like the new norm on a college campus. I've come to expect to meet a new "Brian"—someone who grew up in church but stopped going while in college—every time I step on a college campus. Students with strong Christian faith are increasingly harder to find, while students with little faith (like mine when I was in college) or no faith at all are becoming more commonplace.

Since Christians with weak faith often aren't living out their beliefs, hypocrisy is also a growing dilemma with young adults. More and more, the lack of Christian credibility is keeping skeptics away. In fact, young skeptics between sixteen and twenty-nine years of age have recently stated that Christian hypocrisy is a top reason for rejecting Christian faith.[3]

Grandpa Young and the Credibility Problem

If you read my first book, *Authenticity: Real Faith in a Phony, Superficial World*, you may have been shocked by some of the stories of my infamous Grandpa Young. He spent part of my dad's childhood in the state penitentiary for armed robbery, and he was quite a colorful character, to say the least.

My first memory of my grandpa is still clear, despite the fact that I was only four or five years old. Whenever Grandpa smoked a cigarette and threw it on the ground, my cousins and I always raced to see who could stomp it out first. We pushed and shoved, giggling as we tried to smother its spark.

One Fourth of July my parents, aunts, and uncles socialized in the house playing pinochle while Grandpa enjoyed his usual cigarette break as he watched his grandkids playing outside. Grandpa loved to play tricks, and feeling feisty, he lit an M-80 firecracker and threw *it* (instead of his usual cigarette butt) on the ground. In those days, M-80s were legal, but they have since been banned in the United States due to their power and danger.

"Stomp out that cigarette, boys!" Grandpa exclaimed.

Being the fastest of the cousins, I tore across the yard to stomp Grandpa's "cigarette." Right as my foot approached the ground, I heard the loudest *BOOOOOM!*

For the next few minutes, I only heard ringing in my ears, and I couldn't feel my leg. My cousins gathered around me, concerned. I recognized they were asking me questions, but I couldn't hear any words. One mouthed, "Chad, are you okay?" Thankfully, my hearing eventually returned. That was the last cigarette I would ever stomp out.

My dad recently recalled another story of one of his childhood fishing trips with his father that showed his "feistiness." They floated in an inflatable boat on Lake Erie one summer day with Grandpa's friend Robert. When Robert complained of the summer heat, Grandpa looked at my dad and said, "Can you swim, boy?"

After my dad, who was six or seven at the time, responded by saying he could, Grandpa exclaimed, "Swim, boy!!"

Grandpa then pulled out a large Bowie knife, raised it high in the air, and brought it down into the inflatable boat.

The boat, motor, and hundreds of dollars' worth of fishing gear sank to the bottom of Lake Erie while Robert, Grandpa, and my dad struggled to swim to shore. My dad counts it as one of his many near-death experiences involving Grandpa Young.

I trusted my grandpa, despite the fact that he could have gone to jail for child endangerment many days. I know you are probably reading this thinking, "Chad, you shouldn't have trusted him." Why did I? Because I loved my grandpa and I knew he loved me. Actually, all my cousins loved Grandpa and had faith in him. Some of the adults wanted to trust him, but they felt they had too much to lose. They were worried for their children's safety.

To many of us, Christian faith can resemble my family's faith in my Grandpa Young. You may desire to believe that God exists and that he sent his Son Jesus to rescue the world. Part of you wants to believe the best of Christians. Do you find the teachings of Jesus hard to trust? Do you think Christians are always credible? Do you ever wonder, *What if it's all a sham*?

You may find it comforting to know you're not the first person to find it hard to believe in Jesus, and your generation isn't the first to struggle with Christian faith. People have struggled with it since the very beginning. While many of Jesus' most devout followers died for their faith *after* they witnessed his resurrection, some followers of Jesus in his day struggled to believe in him. Some were on the fringe, choosing not to be "all in" in regard to their faith, and when Jesus' teaching became hard to believe, they simply walked away.

The Reality of "Fringers" and Faith

As a teen, I wasn't "all in" when it came to Christian faith. I guess one could say I lived on the fringe, having marginal views of Christianity. Yes, I did attend church, believed there was a God, and generally tried to be a "good Christian guy." Did I regularly, if ever, pray or read the Bible outside of church? Hardly. I felt guilty about my lack of faith.

My lifestyle and choices didn't reflect the life of Christ, either. I had destructive habits that I just couldn't seem to break. While I wouldn't have admitted it at the time, I mirrored the hypocrite Jonathan Edwards described in his book *Religious Affections*.[4] Edwards claimed if people say they believe something but don't live it out, they don't really believe it.

Edwards went on to say that if there were no heart belief and only intellectual belief, one wouldn't live out one's faith. In other words, we live our lives based on our hearts' affections. As a teen, I possessed intellectual belief in God but lacked heart belief.

According to the Barna research group, teenage Christian "fringers" (like me) are becoming the norm. In their most recent study, published in David Kinnaman's *You Lost Me*, 59 percent of young people with a Christian background report that they have stopped attending church after going regularly, 57 percent say they are less active in church today compared to when they were fifteen, and 38 percent say they have gone through a period when they significantly doubted their faith. Another 32 percent describe a period when they felt like rejecting their parents' faith.[5]

One might be surprised to discover the first Christian "fringers" showed up early on during the ministry of Jesus. How could this be? You might ask how, seeing Jesus, they wouldn't be "all in."

In John 6, Jesus gave some teaching that was difficult to understand and hard to accept. He said, "I tell you the truth, unless you eat the flesh of the Son of Man and drink his blood, you have no life in you. Whoever eats my flesh and drinks my blood has eternal life, and I will raise him up at the last day" (John 6:53–54 NIV 1984). Essentially, he was saying that receiving Jesus was the only way that someone could have eternal life.

> When many of his disciples heard it, they said, "This is a hard saying; who can listen to it?"
>
> But Jesus, knowing in himself that his disciples were grumbling about this, said to them, "Do you take offense at this? Then what if you were to see the Son of Man ascending to where he was before? It is the Spirit who gives life; the flesh is no help at all. The words that I have spoken to you are spirit and life. But there are some of you who do not believe." (For Jesus knew from the beginning who those were who did not believe, and who it was who would betray him.) And he said, "This is why I told you that no one can come to me unless it is granted him by the Father."
>
> After this many of his disciples turned back and no longer walked with him. (John 6:60–66)

Here in John 6 we find the first Christian fringers—Jesus' disciples, struggling to believe his claim that he was the only way to eternal life, which was a complete contradiction to what they had believed all their lives.

At times I've struggled with the same lack of belief. Jesus claimed he is the only way to heaven, but is he? *There can't just be one true religion*, I often thought during my teen years.

There Can't Just Be One True Religion

Is the Christian faith valid? Is it the only true religion? What if the only reason I have Christian faith is because I grew up in a Christian environment? What if everything I've ever been taught about God is a sham?

What's interesting about these common questions is that while many Americans have asked them at some time in their lives, hardly anyone in predominantly Muslim countries doubts there can be just one true religion. In fact, one of the most common beliefs in the Middle East about Christian faith is: "The Christian faith can't be true because so many Americans believe it."

As I've struggled with these questions myself, I've concluded that there is no intellectual integrity to the belief that all religions are equally true. It's the weakest "green biscuit" of all. The only way every religion is equally valid is if there is no God or if God is impersonal.

I think these questions are so common today because of the popularity of relative inclusivism—the assertion that no human being has ever gained absolute truth, but that all human beings have partially attained absolute truth.

This belief is emphasized in the famous poem by John Godfrey Saxe, "The Blind Men and the Elephant." In this poem, Saxe shared the story of six blind men describing an elephant. One touched the elephant's trunk and said the elephant was like a snake. Another touched the tusk and said the elephant was like a spear, and another grabbed the elephant's leg and said the elephant was like a tree. Each man had a different interpretation of the elephant because he was blind and was only touching part of the elephant.

The problem with the poem is that although it appears to be inclusivism on the surface, it's actually covert exclusivism. The poet is telling us that each blind man's interpretation was equally valid, but what he really means is that no one's interpretation is valid but his. He (the author) is the only one who isn't blind and can see the whole elephant.

In the same way, someone may say all religions are equally valid, but they really mean that no one's belief is valid except theirs.

Perhaps you don't believe all religions are equally valid, but you still have problems specifically with the Christian faith. Perhaps you have questions that, like "green biscuits," make you sick of hearing about Jesus.

As I've searched for answers to questions like these, I've discovered that the ultimate answer lies in the person of Jesus of Nazareth. If what he said about himself in John 6 is true (that he is the only way to God—through his death for our sins and his resurrection on the cross), then the Christian faith is the only faith. If he's not who he said he is, then the Christian faith is a sham.

In the next few chapters, I'll continue to share my struggles with Christian faith, and by the end of the book, we'll come back to Jesus' resurrection, the cornerstone of the Christian faith. But first, let's explore the most common struggle that young people have with Christian faith—the problem of evil and suffering.

Notes

[1] David Kinnaman, *You Lost Me: Why Young Christians Are Leaving Church and Rethinking Faith* (Grand Rapids: Baker Books, 2011), 11.

[2] Ibid., 23–24.

[3] David Kinnaman and Gabe Lyons, *unChristian: What a New Generation Really Thinks about Christianity . . . and Why It Matters* (Grand Rapids: Baker Books, 2007), 27.

[4] Jonathan Edward, *A Treatise Concerning Religious Affections* (Dublin: J. Ogle, 1812), Kindle edition.

[5] Kinnaman, *You Lost Me*, 23–24.

CHAPTER ~10~

When Darkness Fell

One night just over three years ago, I witnessed the most brutal attack on a person that I've ever seen.

Driving home from a fundraising event in North Charleston, South Carolina, I passed a young man walking behind a woman. The man was about 6 feet 2 inches, an African American. While it was very dark, his plain white T-shirt reflected in my car lights. The young Caucasian woman walked along in a nonchalant way, oblivious that someone was following her. Meanwhile, the large young man was walking with purpose. Only fifteen feet behind the lady, he appeared to be preparing to overtake her.

It's hard putting it into words, but there was something about the scene that sent shivers up my spine. Kind of like a sixth sense, I could just feel that something evil was taking place.

Right after I passed the woman, I looked in my rearview mirror and saw the woman look over her shoulder at the man and start running. In the dark I saw him catch up to her and attack her, hitting her head and throwing her to the ground.

Instantly, I decided to turn the car around and help the woman. I didn't think about what I'd do when I approached the man in my car, but something inside me said I *had* to turn around. I really didn't stop to think of my own safety or that I had four young children at home. I just remember praying, "Well Lord, I guess this is it." I felt mentally prepared for whatever was about to take place.

As I drove back to where the man and woman were, I laid on my horn in an attempt to scare the man away. When they came into the view of my headlights, the man was dragging the woman by her hair across the street. He walked slowly, as if he was taking his time. The back of the woman's legs bounced across the pavement, as both of her hands clutched the man's hand that was dug into her hair. She was flailing and screaming.

When he realized that I was speeding back toward him, the man abruptly released the woman and sprinted into the darkness. The lady shot up from the street, dashed to my car, and jumped into the passenger's seat. In hysterics, with blood dripping down her head and face, she screamed, "He was going to kill me! I could see it all happening. He told me he was going to kill me!! You ****** saved my life!!"

I asked the young lady, who I could now tell was in her twenties, if I should call the cops or take her to the emergency room.

To that, she exclaimed, "No!!! Please just take me home! Get out of here! He put a gun to my head and said he was going to ***** kill me!!"

I thought it would be better to call 911. Against my better judgment, I complied with her request and drove away from that scene quickly. The young lady, call her Julie, thanked me again and again for turning my car around and coming back for her, and she then directed me to "her house."

North Charleston has one of the highest crime rates in the country, and we were not headed into a safe territory by any means. After a half mile of driving in one of the more dangerous parts of town, we approached a dilapidated trailer. The trailer appeared to have been burned, and the door was missing.

"Is this where you live?" I asked.

Julie answered, "Yes, just let me off here. You need to get out of here, though." She then gave me a big hug, thanked me again, and slipped out of the car. She was still crying hysterically.

Although I didn't call the police that night, the next morning my wife Elizabeth convinced me to file a police report. A woman who was a police officer followed me to the trailer where I dropped off Julie the night before. As we pulled into the driveway, a woman (who wasn't Julie) took off running into the woods. Two shady-looking men stood in front of another trailer behind the burned-out one.

As I opened my car door, I heard the police officer calling for back-up. She said, "Mr. Young, you need to get out of here right now. This isn't a safe place for you. I have help on the way." I immediately followed her order, confident that the situation would be left in the hands of law enforcement.

While my family lived in a safe neighborhood, it shook me to realize how close by us violent acts and crimes took place. Of course, any viewing of the eleven o'clock news is a reminder that there truly is evil in the world.

The problem of evil hindered me from trusting in God over the years. How can a loving God allow evil and suffering in the world? If God is so powerful, why doesn't he put an end to it?

Over the past decade, as I've worked in full-time college ministry, I've witnessed nearly every student wrestle with those very same questions. And I have to admit—I get it. I can totally see how they would question this.

I still struggle with the good-versus-evil issue sometimes. And that's why I know this is not something to be taken lightly.

My Logical Problem with Evil

Can God and evil both exist? I once thought it was logically impossible. If one existed, then the other could not. My struggle was that if God were all-powerful, he could create any kind of world he wanted to. If God were all loving, then he'd prefer a world without evil and suffering. Because suffering exists, there must not be an all-powerful and all-loving God. I wrestled long and hard with this before I was able to find the truth that God and evil do coexist in our world.

My conclusion, after much prayer and study, was that it's not a contradiction to say that God exists in a world where so much evil and suffering take place.

Like so many others and me, though, you may be asking, "How is it logical that God exists at the same time that evil and suffering exist?"

Before I could answer that question, I needed to understand how evil entered the perfect world that God created. I discovered that before God created mankind, he had created angels. One of those angels—the one we know as Satan—brought evil into God's world when he convinced one-third of the other angels to worship him as god.

The Bible describes the battle between God and Satan when the angel Michael led the remaining faithful angels to defeat Satan. Satan and his followers were cast from heaven to earth. Satan changed his tactic to trickery and lies when he took on the form of a serpent in the Garden of Eden. He convinced Adam and Eve to disobey God by eating from the Tree of Knowledge.

The Bible depicts Adam and Eve's choice to disobey God as the birth of humanity's sinful nature. Since then, Satan and his followers have used deception and lies to tempt humans in every generation to commit acts that continue the rift between God and humanity.

The conclusion I reached is this: God did create the world he wanted, a world free from sin, but he created us with free will. He wanted us to choose to love him, just as he gave the angels that same choice. Some of the angels made the wrong choice, and then so did Adam and Eve. That's what brought evil into the world.

God gives each of us the choice to love or not to love him, to live by his commandments or not to live by them. Many people think God is a killjoy with multiple lists of dos and don'ts—that he does not want them to have any fun.

You've heard this before, right? You know what I'm talking about.

The second question I wrestled with involved pain, suffering, and well-being in the presence of an almighty, loving God. I wondered, *Doesn't God prefer a world without suffering? If so, why does he allow it?*

Good and evil as well as well-being and suffering will always exist together in a world with free choice. Both have been the consequences of human choices since Adam and Eve.

Also, there are some mysteries in our world that we will never find a scientific answer for. My answer is that God could have overriding reasons for allowing suffering in the world—reasons I may never understand simply because I'm not all knowing like he is. I am prepared to struggle with this mystery in the midst of my faith.

The reason I can accept the existence of evil and suffering alongside a loving God is because I've come to know God better. Because I know him and understand the depth of his love for humanity, I don't need every question answered. I trust him.

To say my son Clark hates getting shots is a massive understatement. He is so fearful of them that he about makes himself sick with worry over just the possibility of them whenever he visits the doctor. He lacks the perspective that the two seconds of pain will prevent him from weeks of misery that a disease they prevent would bring. No amount of reasoning helps. He just can't see beyond the immediate discomfort.

Like Clark, we don't always know what will be good for us in the end or what God will help us through as we move forward in life. Our perspective is limited. In order for us to see the plans God has for us, he may have to allow suffering in our lives. Even though some suffering is extreme and even though it may be difficult to understand in the near term why God would allow it or why a broken world overwhelms us with evil, it is still logically possible that a great, powerful, and loving God can work things out for our good in the long run (in the eternal big picture).

One example of God working in the midst of suffering involves two dear friends of mine, Gabe and Ryanne O'Sullivan. Their struggle with suffering is quintessential.

Gabe and Ryanne's Story

Gabe and Ryanne O'Sullivan were giddy and excited. After struggling with infertility, Ryanne was pregnant with triplets. When she was twenty-four weeks along, she visited the obstetrician to get the green light to travel to a weekend women's retreat. The doctor discovered she was dilated and in pre-term labor.

Immediately, Ryanne was admitted to the hospital and put on complete bedrest for the remainder of her pregnancy. They had hoped to keep Ryanne from delivering until the babies' lungs could develop, but complications were making that impossible. Ryanne's life was in danger. In order to save Ryanne, the babies had to be delivered at twenty-four and a half weeks.

Reese, Vivian, and Sophia were so small at birth that Gabe could put his wedding band over their hands and slip it all the way to their shoulders. Within the first forty-eight hours, Reese's heart stopped, and the doctors couldn't revive her. A funeral was held for Reese while family and friends held on to the hope that Vivian and Sophia would survive. Two weeks later, Vivian suffered severe brain bleeds and passed away. Ryanne and Gabe again faced another small white casket and another heartbreaking good-bye.

Ryanne and Gabe lived at Sophia's bedside, hoping to bring her home. Sadly, Sophia passed away three months later in the hospital after many ups and downs and after suffering kidney failure. Ryanne and Gabe were grief stricken. They struggled, trying to make sense of how a good God could allow such terrible suffering.

Eight years have passed, and the O'Sullivans have since been blessed with two beautiful children. Gabe wrote a book entitled *Thy Will Be Done?* in which he shares what God has taught him through his experience. I asked Gabe if he'd be willing to share what God has been teaching him. This is what he had to say regarding their losses:

> Every waking moment we weren't talking to Sophia, each other, or someone on the NICU team, Ryanne and I were pleading with God. We begged him to heal our daughter. We asked him to continue being our strength. We were weak, and we needed him to be strong for us. We knew he was the Healer, and we desperately needed him to act in Sophia's favor.
>
> Yet, the more we prayed for our healing, the worse she got. We didn't understand. We thought that when a child of God asks for something that certainly must be within his will, then God was supposed to answer in his or her favor. This was not turning out to be the case, and it hurt us to the core. I realize now that just because we want something and believe our desire must be in God's will does not mean that it is . . . We had to learn that

God's plans are always good, even when we can't see the "good" for the "bad."

As I reflect on Gabe's story and what God has taught me through my own experiences, I'm convinced that relative to the full scope of evidence I see around me, God's existence is more than probable. If suffering is the only thing someone considers when one looks at evidence of whether or not God exists, then maybe his existence seems improbable. However, when he or she looks at the full scope of evidence such as the beauty of creation, the miracle of life, or the existence of good, then God's existence becomes very probable.

In fact, to me the most convincing evidence that God indeed does exist is the existence of both good and evil.

Good and Evil Are Strong Evidence of God's Existence

Many philosophers have thought that morality provides a good argument for God's existence. Consider philosopher William Lane Craig's simple but logical argument in his book *On Guard: Defending Your Faith with Reason and Precision*. He says, "If objective moral values and duties exist, then God exists. Objective moral values and duties do exist. Therefore God exists."[1]

Let me repeat Craig's argument above in my own words: The presence of good and evil in the world is very strong evidence that God exists. Otherwise, where in the world did the idea of good and evil come from?

A few days ago I was talking with a close friend of mine. Call him John for now. John isn't a close follower of Christ. In our discussion, he told me he didn't believe in moral absolutes. He said that anything could be morally right depending on the context. "Even murder can be considered morally good in the right context," John said.

I responded, "Now, John, I've known you for a long time, and because of that I am sure you really believe in moral absolutes. I know that if a child molester were arguing that he was morally right in some cases, you would think he was totally crazy and wrong. I think you believe that molesting children is objectively wrong no matter the circumstances."

John grinned and said, "I concede; there are *some* things that are always wrong. But that doesn't mean that everything is objectively morally right or wrong."

"Okay, John, here's another one," I continued. "Like I said, I know you. If you had money in your pocket for two Happy Meals and passed someone dying of starvation as you were walking into McDonald's, I know that you would buy them a Happy Meal."

John threw his hands up and said, "Okay, that's two examples. Let's just change the subject."

"John," I asked with a smile, "before we change the subject, answer this question. Would you be morally wrong if you didn't feed that person who was starving?"

In order to conclude that God exists, we only have to see that objective moral values exist. According to William Craig, the fact that my friend John has at least some objective moral values is proof that God exists. Otherwise, where does the concept of good and evil come from? On what basis do we define good or evil? Craig would say we could not have established objective moral values through our own natural process.

Here's another way I like to think about this. If we were watching a nature program or Animal Planet, and one animal killed another, we wouldn't call it murder. The only animal that can murder another is a human being—because we're personal beings. Also, when mama sea turtles abandon their young on the beach, we don't accuse them of child abandonment. However, if a human mother abandoned her babies on a beach, it would not be acceptable behavior. As human beings, we have responsibilities that other animals don't have.

I believe that we have responsibilities that other animals don't have because we are created in God's image. Without a God, there would be no basis for good. Humans would be like other animals, rocks, or trees in that there would be no such thing as good or evil.

In the same way, let's consider moral duties. Traditionally our moral duties were thought to spring from God's commandments, such as the Ten Commandments. But if there is no God, what basis remains for moral duties? Think of the sea turtle again. If there were no basis for moral duties other than natural selection, then human mothers would have no duties to their children. They would simply be behaving like mama sea turtles, and abandoning their young would be perfectly acceptable.

Think about some of the moral duties you feel you have toward the earth and mankind. Most young people I've come across recently on campus desire to see sex trafficking end. They're concerned about those who are hungry. They're concerned about the earth and believe we should reduce pollution and invest efforts into conserving our resources. Students hate genocide and other social injustices that are being carried out around the world.

So what are your moral duties? Have you ever stopped to think about where your moral duties come from? In the example I gave earlier, my friend John didn't fully answer me when I asked him about feeding a homeless person with an extra meal from McDonald's, but what would your answer be? Is that part of what Jesus requires of those of us who believe in him and show his love to others?

Without God, we wouldn't have obligations to anyone but ourselves. In fact, I believe that it's the fact of God's existence that causes us to feel these moral duties. I would go so far as to say that without the God of the Bible, we wouldn't have the empathy toward others that we have.

A big advantage that Christian faith has over other world religions is that it offers the best solution to the problem of evil and suffering. A loving God, concerned about humanity, came in the person of Christ to enter into our suffering. Jesus suffered on the cross for us, and if we only place our trust in him and allow him to change our lives, we will one day live life in eternity with no suffering. There's a lot to the kind of life we get to be a part of here in our own corner of the world, but also a greater calling one day that when we die we know we'll be in Heaven with him.

Earlier I told you the story of Julie and her brush with evil one dark night a year ago when that young man attacked her. Julie had been consumed with living her life for herself and thinking of her immediate needs and desires. She hadn't completely surrendered her life to Christ.

As I was driving her home, she was in hysterics, continually repeating, "You saved my life! Thank you! You saved my life!"

At one point I responded to her by saying, "Well, actually *I* didn't save your life. *I* didn't even have to get out of my car. Do you know who *really* saved you?"

Julie responded between her sobs, "No. Who?"

"Jesus did," I said. "I've never been on that street late at night before, and the odds were next to nothing that I'd be there at the same time you were attacked. If I had driven by one minute earlier or one minute later, I never would have seen you. However, Jesus saw you, and he was concerned about you. He had me drive by at just the right second because he wanted to save your life."

Julie dropped her head into her hands and cried out, "Thank you, Jesus! Thank you for saving my life!"

For Julie, a sobering moment in her life highlighted the fact that good and evil do indeed exist. To her, God was concerned about her suffering, and he intervened at just the right second and saved her life amid the darkness. For Julie, God had overcome evil.

How about you? Where do you see God intervening and over-coming the evil that has been around you? Has your response been similar to Julie's? What do you think is needed in order for you to trust in God who does exist in a world that has both good and evil in it?

Earlier in this chapter we explored how evil came into the world, according to the Bible, as one of God's angels tempted Adam and Eve to disobey God's one request. This disobedience caused a rift between God and mankind. A perfectly pure God could no longer be intimate with those Satan corrupted. It would be like perfectly pure water being mixed with dirty water. The pure water would become dirty if you mixed it.

When God removed Adam and Eve from the Garden of Eden, he wasn't just removing them from his presence by kicking them out. God loved his creation. He removed them from the garden so that he could initiate his rescue plan for all the world.

God would send his Son Jesus to provide a way for us to be reunited with him. As Jesus died on the cross for our sins, he took away our impurity. All over the world, people are returning to God. And one day when every nation and tribe has had a chance to hear the gospel, Christ will return to rid the world of evil once and for all.

How does this resonate with you? Do you see opportunities to more fully accept a God who brings good things and allows hard things? What does this mean for you as you take the next step forward?

Note

[1]William Craig, *On Guard: Defending Your Faith with Reason and Precision* (Chicago: David Cook, 2010), Kindle edition.

Shooting Fireworks at Cars Is a Bad Idea

Trouble always found me when my cousin Zach came to visit.

Zach, my first cousin, is a year older than me. Like most kids, to me hanging out with someone a year older was a big deal. I thought Zach was pretty cool, and he had a good bit of influence on me.

In Valley, Alabama, fireworks were legal, and seeing that Zach always visited us on July Fourth and New Year's, fireworks were always present at our gatherings.

After nearly losing my leg in the firecracker incident with Grandpa Young, for a while I was deathly afraid to be near fireworks. Over the years, however, my close encounters with fireworks and my comfort around them increased.

In fact, Zach and I disregarded all the warnings our parents gave us and shot fireworks not only at each other but also at anything else we thought would make a challenging target. We organized fireworks battles with the other cousins and with neighborhood friends. One night my dad even busted us for getting on top of the roof to shoot fireworks at neighbors' houses. We had climbed out a second-floor window, oblivious to the fact that our parents in the house below would hear the commotion.

Yes, we were pretty foolish.

At a family reunion when I was thirteen, Zach suggested, "Let's try shooting some bottle rockets at moving targets . . . like cars."

"Sure!" I responded. Now, Zach's idea scared the heck out of me, but at the time, I was honestly more afraid of Zach than of getting into trouble. As he had grown older, he had grown to be a bit rough. I had seen him attack his older brother on more than one occasion. I didn't want to disappoint or cross Zach, and shooting fireworks at moving targets seemed more desirable than making Zach angry.

We walked a hundred yards to the nearby fireworks stand and purchased one gross of bottle rockets and several Roman candles. After our rooftop incident, we knew we needed to shoot the rockets where my parents wouldn't see or hear us, so we headed to the railroad tracks behind my house. About fifteen feet up a steep incline from the tracks was a four-lane highway with cars traveling forty-five or fifty miles per hour. Come to think of it, we probably looked like two boys from the movie *Stand by Me*.

For the first twenty minutes, Zach and I took turns shooting bottle rockets at passing cars. The odds were slim we'd hit anything. The bottle rockets were difficult to aim, despite launching each one from an empty pop bottle, and the cars were moving too fast. By the time we lit the fuse and aimed the bottle, the car would be past us and too far away.

"This isn't going to work." Zach seemed resigned. "Should we try a Roman candle?"

I hesitated. Bottle rockets were relatively small and created a tiny explosion. Even if a bottle rocket had hit a car, it likely wouldn't have done damage and might not even have been noticed by the driver. Roman candles, on the other hand, shot colored balls of fire. Even in broad daylight, a driver would most definitely notice the fireballs, and because you could hold the Roman candle in your hand and aim, the odds of hitting the mark were exceedingly higher than with the bottle rockets.

By changing our weapon from bottle rockets to Roman candles, I knew we were crossing a line from "just being boys" to being dangerous. "Uh, I don't know," I finally responded. "That seems a bit much. My house is just behind us, and if we get caught, I could get into serious trouble."

Zach waved his hand and reassured me, saying, "Ah, we'll be okay. Besides, I think it will be impossible to hit anything. Those cars are moving too fast. The worst thing that could happen is that we could startle someone and wake the driver up a little. You know, we might even save someone's life by keeping them from falling asleep at the wheel."

I swallowed my hesitations and gave in to Zach. It wasn't the first time he convinced me to do something dangerous, and it wouldn't be the last. I held a Roman candle in my hand and motioned for Zach to light the fuse.

Once Zach lit the match, time seemed to move in slow motion. As the fuse burned to the end, I aimed the firework at an old red Ford F-150 driving on the highway toward us. The Roman candle bucked in my hand as a loud FWOOOM sound split the air. I had a sick feeling in my stomach as the red ball of fire shot toward the red truck.

In my entire life, I have never had a better aim in baseball, rifle shooting, or any other sport than I had that day with the Roman candle. The red fireball hit the driver's side of the windshield, and

I watched in horror as the truck fishtailed and screeched to a sideways halt. I still held the Roman candle upright in my hand, oblivious that there were still seven balls of fire to be shot before the firework extinguished itself.

Zach and I looked at each other with eyes wide in disbelief. I don't think either one of us had thought ahead to what could happen if we actually hit a car. We were just showing off for each other, trying to prove our manhood.

The red truck straightened out on the road and suddenly began racing toward us. The driver had most likely spotted the colored fireballs still shooting upward from where we crouched beside the highway.

When I looked to Zach to ask what to do, he was gone. He had disappeared into the woods. I took off after him, and just before I reached the trees, I heard the truck screech to a stop behind me and the angry driver yelling, "Git back here, you kids!" I never looked back.

Zach and I raced through the woods back to my home. We forgot that if the man followed us, he could have easily detected where I lived and called the cops. Fortunately for us, we never heard from him again.

Looking back on this event, I feel sick when I think how foolish we were to intentionally shoot fireworks at moving cars. We could've easily caused multiple accidents and even fatalities, and Zach and I could have gotten arrested. I shudder as I think of what could've happened and how fortunate the drivers were that day, not to mention us as well.

Most adults would agree that some things are absolutely morally wrong. Shooting balls of fire at moving cars is morally wrong no matter how fun or cool an idea teens might think it is. Most parents would say that my behavior and Zach's that night fall right into that category.

Yet one of the main reasons young people are rejecting Christian faith today is that they want to decide what's morally right or wrong. They don't want others, including their government, teachers, the church, or especially the Bible, telling them what they should or should not do. Young people feel it's their right to determine their own moral values, and this right is absolutely sacred to them. It's what makes them feel genuine.

"I'm Not Genuine Unless I Decide What's Right"

This past summer, I took several graduate classes in Ft. Collins, Colorado, at Colorado State University. My philosophy class final project required that I interview CSU students and faculty to learn their world views. How do they define happiness? What is their philosophy of life? What makes a person successful? Are there any objective standards of right or wrong? What makes a person a good person? These are examples of questions I asked in my interviews.

I met Ada and Sarah one afternoon during lunch in the CSU student center. Both girls were sophomores who had grown up in Ft. Collins before entering college there. Ada appeared Middle Eastern in descent and wore the head covering of a Muslim woman. I desired to get feedback from students from as many different ethnic backgrounds as possible, so I was eager to hear Ada's thoughts. While there are few minority groups in Ft. Collins, a relatively large population of Muslim families lives there.

As the two girls were finishing their lunch, I approached and asked if they could take a short survey for the project. Both students seemed delighted to help out. Ada wore blue jeans and a blouse similar to what Sarah was wearing. Only her red headdress stood out between the two of them. Ada offered to take the survey first.

"Great," I responded. "I'll ask you some questions, and then I'll ask Sarah the same questions. First of all, Ada, how would you describe happiness?"

Ada replied, "I'd say being happy means you're not worried about much. One who's happy can get through anything. As long as you're happy most of the time, you're able to move forward in life."

I continued asking Ada questions, and at one point I asked about her view of God:

Ada claimed to believe in the existence of one God, but she admitted she doesn't live her life thinking much about it. She said, "I don't really worry much about God or really anything else. I really don't even care about school or learning anything at all. Life is about finding happiness, and if you're happy most of the time, then you've achieved a successful life."

After analyzing what Ada said about success, happiness, and God, it was easy to conclude that although she grew up in a Muslim family, Ada didn't live her life based on her family's beliefs. She believed the individual decides what success is or what brings happiness in life. God existed, but to Ada he was a bystander that wasn't involved in our everyday lives. Ada's central goal in life was to be happy, as Ben Franklin often said, and to feel good about herself.

Sarah's views were similar to her friend Ada's. When I asked Sarah about her philosophy of life or what she lived by, she replied, "I just live my life based on what makes me happy. I personally don't know if there's a God, and I don't think that's ultimately important. We should all live life trying to be good to others, and generally it's up to us to decide what's good and what's not."

Ada and Sarah represent the new norm on college campuses around the country. Today the typical young person is content with not knowing whether or not there is a God. They place a higher value on being genuine than on being religious, and their mantra is: "I'm not genuine unless I decide what's right or what's wrong."

This generation has a hard time with a God who tells them what to do. They despise a Bible that defines sexual immorality and tells them how to live their lives. Their right to choose what's right is sacred, and to many, it has become the number one barrier keeping them from pursuing God.

Two Important Points Concerning Sacredness of Choice

If you're in Ada and Sarah's shoes, there are at least two things that I want to share with you to help you to overcome your barrier to knowing God. The first is a question: Is anyone in the world doing something that is morally wrong even though they think it's right?

There are many examples of crimes committed by people without moral conviction. Child molestation and human trafficking are obvious examples. My story of shooting Roman candles at moving cars is another one, although it is a much lighter example than the previous two.

Remember the conversation I had with my friend John. When he argued that no moral absolutes exist, I made him admit that he thinks child molestation is wicked. He wound up having to agree with me that "some things are always wrong." It would be a rare person indeed who doesn't think so.

This leads to the second point, which is that everyone must live for something. Some live for family, while others live for their careers, relationships, sex, popularity, video games, sports, God, social networking, or money. For most of us, the focus jumps around from one thing to another. We may live for social networking one day and for a dating relationship the next.

Whatever we live for the most becomes our master and lord. If we live too much for sports, then that can become our master. We can become obsessed with exercising or dreaming about being a professional athlete. If we spend too much time playing video games or social networking, they can become our masters. God made us so that we seem to be hardwired to crave a master. When our favorite activities dominate our thoughts, then they take the place of our Lord.

I've found that the concept of having a master and lord really resonates with many students. Most waste countless hours daily on the Internet, and many students spend significant time daydreaming and worrying about relationships. Many underestimate the power that any master can have over our lives.

When we can understand the concept that we all serve something that is the lord and master over us, the gospel can become powerfully clear to us. As Becky Pippert said, Jesus is the only master that will fulfill you, and if you fail him, he died for you. Any other master will leave you wanting.[1]

Many times I've had other masters besides God in my life. Growing up, sports and earning good grades were my masters. I had several girlfriends in high school, and each of those relationships spent time as my master. In fact, at some time in my life, I've probably had just about every master one can have. So I know from experience that only God has been a master in whom I've found fulfillment.

Another example that hits close to home involves my sister-in-law's ex-husband, Keith. Years ago, Keith left my sister-in-law, Mary Irene, to pursue other masters in his life. For years, he had gone to bars with his buddies several nights a week while Mary Irene stayed home with the kids. He finally found a relationship with another woman and divorced Mary Irene. For years, Keith continued dating other women while neglecting his two kids and often being verbally abusive to Mary Irene.

But then something happened two years ago that changed everything. One Tuesday night, after Keith returned home from drinking with his friends, he had a stroke in his living room. He was partially paralyzed and couldn't move, and he lay there helpless on the floor from Tuesday through Sunday.

By Sunday, Mary Irene had become very worried because she hadn't been able to reach Keith. When he wouldn't answer the door, police and paramedics were called and arrived at his house. They found him near death, lying right next to his phone, which had a dead battery. He spent a few weeks in the hospital and received intense physical therapy. Eventually Keith was able to walk and moved into a rehab center.

Mary Irene was a Christ figure in Keith's life. Although he had treated her poorly for many years and had left her and the boys, Mary Irene forgave him completely. Keith had no other family willing to oversee his care, so Mary Irene helped to take care of him. For the past two years, she has picked him up nearly every Friday, and she brings him to her house for the weekend so he can spend time with his boys.

When Keith and Mary Irene were married, Keith refused to go to a Protestant church. Now she takes him to church every Sunday, and he enjoys the worship. He's joyful throughout each service and looks forward to it. Before the stroke, Keith neglected to spend quality time with his sons. Now he savors every moment with them and constantly hugs and tells them he loves them.

When I first heard about Keith's transformation, I wasn't sure if I believed it. During the several years I knew him when he and Mary Irene were together, he didn't even speak to me at family gatherings, not even when I tried to talk to him. I didn't fully believe Keith had changed until I spent time with him a year or so ago at a Thanksgiving family gathering.

Keith and I were watching a Clemson-South Carolina rivalry game, and ESPN was showing a clip of an awful knee injury to South Carolina's star running back, Marcus Lattimore, earlier in the season.

Keith, who has permanent brain damage and has had some difficulty communicating since his stroke, looked over at me and said, "Ouch!"

I nodded to him and said, "That's right. That was a very painful injury. That's too bad for Marcus." In the sixteen or so years that I had known Keith, this was my first real conversation with him.

Keith pulled up his pant leg and showed me where he had scars from a knee surgery. "Ouch!" he said. "That hurt him. Too bad."

I then pulled up both of my pant legs and showed Keith the scars from my ten knee surgeries. Like Marcus Lattimore and Keith, I had suffered, too.

Keith looked at my knee and grimaced. "Ouch!" he said again. "I'm sorry for you."

It was then that I realized that for the first time in many years, Keith had empathy. He had empathy for Mary Irene. He had empathy for his two sons as well as for me and my knee problems, and he even had empathy for a South Carolina football player.

Our family believes in miracles, and we believe that in Keith we've seen one with our own eyes. God works in mysterious ways, and only he can change the heart of a man or a woman. If we can surrender our hearts completely to him and allow Christ to be our Lord and Master, we will find joy and fulfillment beyond our comprehension.

In the previous three chapters, we've discussed three "green biscuits" that are making young people sick of the Christian faith, and one could say these first three green biscuits are influenced by the culture around us. Now let's take a look at the green biscuit that Christians must take responsibility for. It's the green biscuit of the poor track record of Christians.

Note

[1]Becky Pippert, *Out of the Salt Shaker and into the World: Evangelism as a Way of Life* (Westmont, IL: InterVarsity Press, 1999), Kindle edition.

CHAPTER ~12~

A Death-Defying Stunt on Thrill Hill

When I was sixteen, I had one of those moments behind the wheel of a car when your whole life flashes before your eyes in an instant.

My dad had just gotten me a 1984 TransAm with a T-top roof. Well, it was debatable whom the car actually belonged to. Dad said it was his dream car, but I was the one who usually got to drive it. The amazing metallic brown muscle machine with a 305 engine could fly. I was in the tenth grade and tutored a couple of sixth-grade boys in math and a couple of other subjects. We jumped in my car every day after school and headed toward the house of Matt, one of the boys.

Between Springwood School and Matt's house was one of the steepest hills I've ever driven down. Most teenagers in Lanett, Alabama, referred to it as "thrill hill." One could easily elevate off the ground simultaneously all four tires of just about any car if the right speed was reached in time. Every day I took the boys down thrill hill, and we whooped and hollered all the way down. In hindsight, I gambled my life and the lives of those boys every day that we made the trip. It was stupid.

On one particular day, I stopped the car fifty yards from the top of the hill and revved my engine. The boys yelled, "Go-Go-Go," and I yanked my foot off the brake. When we reached the crest of the hill, we elevated and found ourselves in midair staring down the hill. At that moment, a woman in a red Buick reached a stop sign near the bottom of the hill. She never stopped or looked at the car that was speeding right at her.

When all four of my wheels finally hit the pavement, I hit the brake hard, but it was too late. The car spun out of control, barely missing the Buick but wrapping itself around a telephone pole on the side of the road. Everything went black.

As I slowly regained consciousness several minutes later, I found the windshield buckled over my head. The telephone pole pressed next to my right leg. The passenger seat was a mangled mess, and the floorboard below the seat had disappeared. My first thought was, *Where's Matt?*

Fortunately for all of us, no one was killed that day. Matt, who didn't have his seatbelt on, was thrown from the car but suffered only a broken arm. The other boy in the backseat had been wearing a seatbelt and was uninjured. I had a bad concussion and lacerations from broken glass, but my seatbelt had saved my life. I was unaware that Matt wasn't wearing his seatbelt, but had he been wearing it, he wouldn't have survived the crash. We were beyond lucky.

Needless to say, Matt's parents didn't trust me to drive their son home after that. I didn't blame them. I hadn't treated their son as precious cargo. Having had my driver's license for only a few months, I didn't have much credibility. My driving record would forever be tarnished in their eyes.

Sadly, many young people today don't trust Christians because many of our "life-driving" records are tarnished, much like mine was after my car accident. In fact, according to the Barna Group, a whopping 85 percent of young adults between the ages of sixteen and twenty-nine who don't follow Christ view Christians as hypocrites,[1] saying there is a disconnect between what we say we believe and how we live our lives.

People who don't follow Christ aren't the only ones affected by poor driving records. Young Christians, the ones who are doing the "poor driving," are also hurt by their own hypocritical lifestyles. In fact, thousands of college freshmen that were passionate for God in high school can't be found in a church or a Bible study while in college. As a matter of fact, one can see little evidence of their Christian faith in the choices they make.

Christians Have a Bad Driving Record

Recently, during a visit to the University of Georgia, I ate lunch in one of the cafeterias on campus with a friend named Josh. I currently coach the team of nine full-time UGA staff with Cru, a college ministry. I travel there to spend time with them on a regular schedule.

Josh and I struck up a conversation with Paul, who was also eating lunch. As we talked to Paul, we learned he was a member of a social fraternity on campus. We soon realized some of Paul's closest friends were great guys involved in our campus ministry. I asked Paul if he'd ever been to a weekly Cru meeting or a Bible study.

Paul responded, "No, I haven't yet, but I plan on it. A lot of my friends have said great things about Cru, and those guys in my fraternity Bible study are awesome. I just haven't felt right about joining their study group."

"Why is that?" I prodded.

"To be honest with you, Chad, I've been having too much fun," he said. "Look, I know my lifestyle in college and my relationship with my girlfriend haven't been right in God's eyes. I've been to church all my life, was one of the main leaders of my youth group, and even thought at one point God was calling me to be a missionary. But things have changed. At some point, I want to go back to being on fire for God because I know how happy I was then. I just know I can't be as good as those other Christian guys in my fraternity. I've destroyed my reputation as a Christian already, and I don't want to mess up the great ministry they have going on right now."

I could tell Paul was beating himself up for messing up his relationship with God, and he didn't need me to beat him up even more. I did, however, remind him of one of God's truths.

"Paul," I said, "God has big plans for you, bigger than you can ever imagine. Who knows? He may even have plans for you to be a missionary if that's what he was laying on your heart in high school. You know how happy you were then, and I can tell you're frustrated with your lifestyle now. Don't wait too much longer to get things right with God. If you do, you might miss out on the adventure he has planned."

Paul and I ended our conversation on a good note, and he promised me he would seek out the other Christian guys in his fraternity and get involved in their Bible study.

You may be in Paul's shoes right now, frustrated with yourself because your "Christian driving record" hasn't been so great. If not, you probably know someone who is in Paul's shoes. If you do, I'd encourage you to have a heart-to-heart conversation with them. It's critical that someone who loves them reminds them that God has a plan for their lives. Further, because God is patient, merciful, and full of grace, he's always ready to welcome you back to his glorious road. My dad is a good example of that.

My dad became a follower of Christ as a teenager and told his church counselor when he was fourteen that God was calling him into full-time Christian ministry. He wasn't a bad person, but sports, college, and fun began to cloud his vision, and he developed a "poor Christian driving record." He lost track of his commitment to God and all but forgot some of his early promises he made to God.

Over time, my dad graduated from college, married my mother, and found a great job selling boats in his father-in-law's marine store. He and my mother started a family, began to attend church, and were enjoying a good life in Wooster, Ohio.

One day a family entered the marine store to purchase a boat and uttered a few words that brought my dad back to God's plan. My dad was using sign language to communicate with one of the family's deaf children, and the mother noticed.

After observing the conversation, the mother asked my dad, "Where did you learn to sign?"

My father smiled and told her that he had interpreted for the deaf families who attended his church when he was a teenager. The woman then spoke the few words that brought my dad back to his spiritual senses and the vision God had given Dad at that church camp fifteen years earlier: "What are you wasting your life selling boats for?"

Of course, there's nothing wrong with selling boats for a living. My grandfather had done it for most of his career, but my dad understood in that moment that for him it was wasting his life because God had called him to do something else. Within a few months, he entered seminary and has forever been thankful for the "woman sent from God to wake me up and remind me of God's plan," as he puts it. This year he celebrates being a minister for thirty years.

You may be the one to utter the exact words that will help another get on God's right path, or perhaps you're even reading this right now thinking, *Hey, when I was younger I believed God was calling me to* _____ , *but I've sort of gotten off track like your dad*. It's never too late to get back on track.

One of the most common conversations I have with students who don't claim to have a relationship with Christ centers on the fact that they don't trust Christians. Amanda at Colorado State despised Christianity because most of her friends who were Christians were hypocrites. Kristen at the College of Charleston quit going to church while she was in college because she felt her Christian friends were the hardest partiers. The list goes on and on and on. I've probably had over a hundred conversations in my last fourteen years of college ministry with students who had been burned by Christian hypocrisy.

When I get into a conversation regarding Christian hypocrisy, I've learned to have one main goal in the conversation: I try to be the very best ambassador for Christ that I possibly can be.

Being Christ's Ambassador

There is no winning an argument with someone who has been turned off from Christian faith by hypocrisy in the church. The reputation of Christ in their eyes has already been tarnished before the conversation begins. That's why it's important to realize that God has chosen us to be his ambassadors.

It's an honor and privilege, but sometimes it's not pretty. We are called to step into situations when others are confused and looking for answers. Sometimes being Christ's ambassador requires us to allow someone who's angry to vent his or her frustrations on us.

When I remember that I'm Christ's ambassador and that the conversation isn't about me, it helps me to be the right kind of listener with empathy toward the person I'm talking to. I can be calm and understanding because ultimately they're not angry with me. They're angry with God because of the way they've been treated or what they've seen in the people who are supposed to be following him.

When Amanda at Colorado State told me she walked away from the church because of Christian hypocrisy, I said, "You know, Amanda, I'm really sorry. You see, when I was in high school and even a freshmen in college, I called myself a Christian but didn't act like it. I was very hypocritical in my lifestyle, and I probably hurt some people in the same way that you were hurt. In fact, I know that I did. I never got a chance to apologize to most of those folks because they weren't lengthy friendships, but I'd love to apologize to you now on behalf of your high school friends. Amanda, would you forgive me for my past hypocrisy?"

Amanda did forgive me, and before our conversation ended, the last thing she told me was, "Maybe there is something real about genuine Christian faith."

Being Christ's ambassador in Amanda's life was pretty straight-forward. I just loved her, cared for her, and listened to her the way that Christ would. Sometimes, however, conversations can be more difficult.

I've had conversations with many sharp students who know that there were some dark days in the history of the church, and these were the hardest conversations to have. Undoubtedly, two times in church history that are brought up are the dark days of the Crusades, when some vicious church people ruled in Europe, and the days when many Christians promoted slavery and slave trade.

Again, when I have these conversations, my main goal is just to be a good ambassador for Christ. As Christians, we have to admit that some Christians, or people who called themselves fol-lowers of Christ, used their power to hurt and take advantage of other people. However, we can also be proud of the fact that godly men and women were responsible for some great events like the

Civil Rights Movement, one of the greatest spiritual movements in American history.

A Call to a Deeper Faith

One of the greatest books I've ever read and one that all followers of Christ should read is *The Autobiography of Martin Luther King, Jr.* King's book details his walk of faith and the passion God gave him to call others to a deeper faith. King wrote, "My parents would always tell me that I should not hate the white man, but that it was my duty as a Christian to love him. The question arose in my mind: How could I love a race of people who hated me and who had been responsible for breaking me up with one of my best childhood friends? This was a great question in my mind for a number of years."[2]

He was born Michael King, but his father later changed his name to Martin Luther King Jr. in honor of the great German reformer Martin Luther. A powerful Baptist preacher, he became a civil rights activist early in his career. While some African American leaders wanted to protest violently, King's faith led him to call others to protest through nonviolent civil disobedience based on Christian faith. In his "I Have a Dream" speech, King talked about his faith in God:

> With this faith, we will be able to hew out of the mountain of despair a stone of hope. With this faith, we will be able to transform the jangling discords of our nation into a beautiful symphony of brotherhood. With this faith, we will be able to work together, to pray together, to struggle together, to go to jail together, to stand up for freedom together, knowing that we will be free one day.[3]

Many years before King helped lead the civil rights movement in America, another strong believer, William Wilberforce, led a movement to abolish slave trade in Europe. Wilberforce was convinced of the importance of religion, morality, and education. He headed the parliamentary campaign against the British slave trade for twenty-six years, until the passage of the Slave Trade Act of 1807. He championed causes and campaigns such as the Society for the Suppression of Vice, British missionary work in India, the creation of a free colony in Sierra Leone, the foundation of the Church Mission Society, and the Society for the Prevention of Cruelty to Animals.

In later years, Wilberforce supported the campaign for the complete abolition of slavery, and continued his involvement after 1826, when he resigned from Parliament because of his failing health. That campaign led to the Slavery Abolition Act 1833, which abolished slavery in most of the British Empire; Wilberforce died just three days after hearing that the passage of the Act through Parliament was assured.

Yes, many Christians like MLK and William Wilberforce have done amazing things to stop social injustice around the world, but we must acknowledge that many Christians have done evil things as well. There's a reason Christians do evil things, and it's found in the Bible.

Why Can't We All Get Along?

One of the most common reasons many young people have been turned off by Christian faith is division in the church. In my twelve years of full-time college ministry, I've had so many conversations about this topic that I've lost count.

Yes, there are many Christian leaders who have fallen, and certain topics have divided many churches. Followers of Christ sometimes argue and fight just like people who aren't followers.

In 2 Samuel 20, we see an example of the people of God being divided over something that seems trivial today. At the end of 2

Samuel 19, David had been brought back to Jerusalem to reclaim his throne after one of his sons temporarily stole it. Half of the people of Israel and all of the people of Judah met David in Mahanaim to escort the king back to Jerusalem, but David left Manahaim before some of the northern tribes, who had the longest distance to travel, could get there. This one little misstep by David would cause an already divided nation to split into two nations of God's people a couple of generations later. It all started when one man, Sheba, said: "We have no portion in David, and we have no inheritance in the son of Jesse; every man to his tents, O Israel!" (2 Sam. 20:1).

I wonder how many church splits were started by just one man's disrespectful, disobedient comment about a pastor or leader in a church. Probably a lot.

The idea that Christians shouldn't fall, fail, or fight is based on a mistaken belief concerning what Christianity teaches about itself. First of all, everything good comes from God (Jas. 1:17). When Christians are good or when they don't fight, it's only because of the work that the Lord has done in their hearts.

Because of the original sin in the Garden of Eden, people have always had a flawed human nature. People, whether they call themselves followers of Christ or not, will always have a desire to be in control, a desire to always be right, and a desire to find joy in other places besides God.

The Bible often speaks about the seriously flawed character of all Christians. It's true that when the Spirit leads a follower of Christ, he or she should have Christlike character. However, at times every Christian stops allowing the Spirit to lead, and when we stop listening to the Spirit, our flawed human nature comes out. Growth is a gradual process; it only occurs when followers of Christ love God and surrender their lives to Jesus regularly. This means the church will be filled with broken people who still have a long way to go emotionally, morally, and spiritually.

The fact that the church is full of broken people also explains why fanaticism is common. When you hear the phrase "religious fanatic," you probably think of someone who's overbearing, self-righteous, opinionated, insensitive, and harsh. Christian fanatics give the church a bad reputation with those who are outside the church, not because they're too passionate about sharing the gospel with others, but because they're not committed enough to the gospel. In other words, Christian fanatics may communicate the gospel to others, but they forget how broken they are themselves and how desperately we all need a Savior.

Remember the parable of the lost sons? The Pharisees that Jesus was addressing were the religious fanatics of the day. He told the parable to show them that they were like the oldest son who was missing out on the father's love. The younger son experienced the father's love because he recognized the depth of his sin and ran to the father.

Why do churches have division? Why do some Christians not get along? Because we're broken. The Bible says we are, and the only way we can keep from having division or keep from falling into sin is by the grace of God.

Now there is at least one other "green biscuit" that keeps young people from experiencing God's love today. I've included it as the last chapter of my book because if this one event happened, it would change everything.

Notes

[1] Kinnaman and Lyons, *unChristian*, 27.

[2] Martin Luther King, Jr., *The Autobiography of Martin Luther King, Jr.* (New York: Warner Books, 1998), 7.

[3] Ibid., 226.

CHAPTER ~13~

It All Comes Down to Easter Sunday

In 1952, a twenty-year-old man entered a mom-and-pop store. The man, sporting a reversible jacket with pop bottle caps glued on the outside, carried a gun. He proudly called himself the "Pop Bottle Kid." He robbed stores while wearing the jacket. As he exited each store, he quickly reversed the jacket so that the shiny bottle caps were hidden. Looking for an armed villain with a shiny jacket, the Ohio police unknowingly let the "Pop Bottle Kid" slip away each time.

On this particular day in 1952, however, the cops caught their perpetrator. They hauled him to the precinct, and later a judge found the Pop Bottle Kid guilty of armed robbery. Police ushered him to the Mansfield Reformatory, where he spent a year in the Ohio prison system.

I knew the Pop Bottle Kid as Grandpa Young, my paternal grandfather. Everything in his life up to his twentieth birthday had led him down a path that could only lead to prison, so no one who knew him was surprised to see him go.

Grandpa Young was born in Hazard, Kentucky. He was one of nine boys, all of them named after famous people. Some of my Grandpa's brothers' names were Christopher Columbus Young, Franklin Delano Young, and Robert Lee Young. My grandpa's legal name on his birth certificate read "G. W.," and everyone assumed he was named after George Washington. Hence, he was called George most of his adult life after he moved from Kentucky to Ohio.

No one knew exactly when Grandpa was born because his birth certificate just indicated he was born on May 39 (yes, you read that correctly—he was the only person ever born on May 39) with no year listed. Perhaps an illiterate hospital worker filled out Grandpa Young's birth certificate after he was born, or maybe it was someone pulling a prank. Many people in Hazard were known to be mischievous.

One ornery family in Hazard, the McCurry family, was full of boys like my grandfather's family. My great-grandfather was a rather mean man. He raised his boys to be tough, but the McCurry boys were apparently known to be a little rougher and tougher. Many days they stole the milk money from my grandpa and his older brothers and chased them home after school. They were bullies.

One day when Grandpa Young was about eight, my great-grand-father caught a glimpse of his sons running from the McCurrys. That afternoon, he sat them down. As he took off his belt, he looked each of them in the eye and sternly declared, "If I ever see you running from those boys again, I'm going to take this belt and whip each of you until you can't sit. Do you hear me?"

Each boy nodded. Although they were afraid of the McCurrys, they were even more fearful of their father.

The following day, during the daily McCurry confrontation, my grandpa and his older brothers stood their ground. A fight ensued that I'm told became legendary in Hazard for many years. My grandpa, only in elementary school at the time, grabbed one of the McCurry boys during the fight and bit off a portion of his ear. Needless to say, the McCurry kids never stole the Young kids' milk money again.

While all the boys were quite a handful, my grandpa and his younger brother Christopher Columbus were the roughest of the bunch. They were in and out of trouble during their teen years. Grandpa married my Grandma Marian when he was eighteen, and soon after that they had their first child, my father, Herb. While my dad was a baby, Grandpa spent a year away in the Mansfield Reformatory. Then, when he was released, his brother Chris continued to find illegal jobs for them.

When my dad was just eight, Grandpa Young and Chris were again arrested after committing a major robbery. This time they broke into a military armory and stole a carload of guns. Although prison sentences then for stealing guns weren't as tough as they are today, my grandpa's stunt eventually landed both him and his brother Chris in the Ohio State Penitentiary.

My grandma never condoned his lifestyle and was never aware of his shenanigans until after the fact. He had told her he was just borrowing her car to run some errands the evening he broke into the armory. Yet, despite his lies, Grandma took her wedding vows seriously. She loved Grandpa for better or for worse, and she forgave him each time he was released from prison.

After Grandpa's release from the state penitentiary, his brother Chris continued to tempt him with illegal jobs, but Grandpa stood firm. A law in Ohio at the time said that if a felon were convicted three times, the third sentence would result in a mandatory lifetime behind bars. Afraid of the consequences of a third conviction, my grandpa decided to be a law-abiding citizen.

Not long after Grandpa was released from prison, his brother Franklin Delano came to know Jesus as his Lord and Savior. Frank encouraged his pastor to share Christ with my grandpa, and when he did, my grandpa also prayed and asked Jesus to come into his life.

It's clear now that at this point, God began to weave a story of redemption into my family tree. My grandpa wasn't perfect after that, as none of us are. However, Grandpa and Grandma Young did start attending church.

My dad, who had never stepped foot into a church building before Grandpa's prison release, heard the gospel for the first time when he was twelve. During his eighth-grade year, Dad received Jesus as his Lord and Savior. Soon after that, my dad says he sensed God calling him to full-time ministry. He has spent his adult career serving God as a pastor or nursing home administrator.

My spiritual journey is directly related to my dad's, of course. Had he not fallen in love with God, I likely would have never written this book.

Now, the key in my family's story is that something took place that changed the trajectory of my dad's life. Was that "something" a supernatural event, or did it simply involve the behavior modification of my grandpa? When people meet my dad and hear of his upbringing, they scratch their heads. How did he come out of such a broken environment and turn out so wonderful? My father is one of the most generous, loving, joyful people I know. I have also always admired my dad for not trash-talking his father or his story. He speaks of him with respect and love. He sees his upbringing as a redemption story, one in which God clearly intervened.

Many people question if God really exists, and if Jesus was truly the Son of God. Many question whether the Christian faith is a sham. My dad is not one of those people, as he saw God work in his life and his family's life in a way that was amazing and life changing. Many continue to ask these questions today, though. The answers to these questions have been debated for centuries and for good reason.

If Jesus really was who he said he was—if he was really God, it changes everything. It means that everything in the Bible is absolutely true. A supernatural God could make sure that biblical authors wrote exactly what he wanted them to write, and he could make sure it was passed down to us without errors.

It would mean that Jesus is the only way to God, just as he said he was. It would mean that there is indeed a Heaven and that good works could never get us there. Having faith in Jesus would be enough to spend eternity with God.

If someone took Jesus to court to prove he wasn't God, and if I were sitting on the jury, there's one event in the life of Jesus I would focus on: his resurrection. If a defense attorney could prove beyond a shadow of a doubt that the resurrection took place, I would believe Jesus was God.

On the flip side, if a prosecuting attorney could prove the resurrection did not take place, it would be apparent that Christian faith is one of the biggest hoaxes the world has ever seen.

Each of us will be faced with that decision at some time in our life or, perhaps, many times. Let's pretend we're on that jury and examine the evidence.

Exploring the Evidence

You may have heard someone say, "Well, you can't prove that Jesus was raised from the dead. That supposedly happened two thousand years ago, and we can't go back in time."

If we believed that, however, we would have no need for a court system. Every day in courts around the world, thousands of lawyers take judges and juries back in time by presenting the evidence, both physical and circumstantial, and by presenting the testimonies of eyewitnesses in their cases.

When a lawyer can use the evidence to prove to a jury beyond a shadow of a doubt that someone is guilty, a verdict is reached, and a sentence is given.

Take the court case in which my Grandpa Young was found guilty of robbing an armory. Although he told my grandma he was guilty, Grandpa pleaded not guilty during the trial.

It was a very short trial. The prosecuting attorney brought one of the three accomplices in the burglary to the witness stand to serve as an informant, and he exposed the truth. He named my grandpa and Grandpa's brother Chris as his accomplices. To thank him for his help, the police dropped all charges against this man, who also gave them the whereabouts of the stolen guns.

Next the defense attorney argued that there was no physical evidence. When the police arrived at the location where the informant said the guns were hidden, no evidence was found. Of course, as Grandpa later told Grandma, he and Chris had already moved the guns just in case the police came looking.

Then the prosecuting attorney reviewed my grandpa's criminal record. He had already served extended time at the Mansfield Reformatory for armed robbery. As they say in the movies, "His rap sheet was as long as he is tall." My grandpa had a bad reputation and track record; the prosecutor knew this trial would be a slam dunk.

The prosecuting attorney's prediction turned out to be right.

In less than an hour, the trial ended. Even without physical evidence, my grandpa was charged with breaking and entering and was sentenced to three years in the Ohio State Penitentiary. He later admitted to my grandma that he was guilty, but he never admitted any guilt in the courtroom.

Imagine that Jesus was being tried in a court of law for being the Son of God. Just as a jury listened to my grandpa's case, we can explore the evidence concerning Jesus' resurrection and reach a verdict of whether or not we believe it really happened.

Evidence for the Resurrection

The first and strongest piece of evidence concerns the empty tomb and the witnesses. Most Bible scholars believe the apostle Paul wrote the very first account of the resurrection of Jesus before any of the four Gospels were written, just fifteen to twenty years after the death of Jesus (while many witnesses to the life of Jesus were still alive).

In 1 Corinthians 15:3–6, Paul wrote,

> For I delivered to you as of first importance what I also received: that Christ died for our sins in accordance with the Scriptures, that he was buried, that he was raised on the third day in accordance with the Scriptures, and that he appeared to Cephas, then to the twelve. Then he appeared to more than five hundred brothers at one time, most of whom are still alive, though some have fallen asleep.

Because Paul's letter was written so soon after Jesus' death and because so many witnesses who had actually seen the resurrected Jesus with their own eyes were still alive at the time, we find very few who would argue with Paul's claim. If Christ had not indeed been raised from the dead, Christianity would have been discredited and ended before Paul's ink was dry.

Anyone in the churches where this public letter was read could have visited one of the eyewitnesses to verify Jesus' resurrection. There were also the four Gospels written by four separate authors, and each one identifies witnesses to the empty tomb and risen Savior.

If a defense attorney argued that Jesus rose from the dead, the second piece of evidence he or she could submit in a courtroom today would be the women's accounts of Jesus' resurrection.

Included in the testimonies of witnesses in the four Gospels were the testimonies of women. In first-century Jewish culture, women had low social status, which meant that their testimony was not admissible evidence in courts of that day. There was no possible advantage to the church to recount that all the first witnesses were women. It could only have undermined the credibility of the testimony.

The only possible explanation for why women were depicted as meeting Jesus first is if they really had. If the Gospel authors wanted to falsify evidence or only pretend that Jesus was raised from the dead, they would have said men were the first to see Jesus. There must have been enormous pressure on the early apostles to omit the women's testimonies, yet I believe they included them because that's exactly how it happened and that is exactly how God wanted his Word to tell it.

The third piece of strong evidence is the explosion of a new world view. When Jesus arrived on the scene, there was a lot of confusion regarding the Messiah and what he would be like. Most Jews had a view that Jesus would come as a king and would rule the earth, returning to King David's glorious kingdom.

In Old Testament Scripture were passages about Jesus being both a lion and a lamb, and there were also passages about Jesus being a servant, born into poverty. However, because the Jews had spent hundreds of years living under the power of pagan and worldly kingdoms, the belief that Jesus would be a king, a ruler, a deliverer, and a lion stood out and gave them hope.

It's clear that the Pharisees doubted that Jesus was the Messiah because he didn't appear to be the king they expected, and even his disciples expected him to rule and not to be crucified.

Then immediately following the crucifixion, the disciples were in hiding because they were confused and in fear of being next in line for crucifixion. However, after they witnessed the resurrected Savior, a new world view involving a risen Savior immediately emerged. As fast as Paul could write it to the believers in Corinth, Rome, and Colossae, he taught that Christ was the firstborn from the dead, and he promised future resurrection to all who believe (1 Cor. 15:20; Rom. 8:11; Col. 1:18).

From that time until now, Christians have had a resurrection-centered view of reality: our future resurrection has already begun in Jesus.

Usually it takes many years for world views to develop, but the Christian view of resurrection, absolutely unprecedented in history, sprang up full-blown immediately after the death of Jesus. There was no process or development. His followers said their beliefs didn't come from debating or discussion. They were simply telling others what they had seen themselves—a resurrected Christ!

Despite the fact that Jesus died two thousand years ago, the evidence supporting his resurrection is overwhelming. The tomb was empty three days after Jesus was buried. What happened to the body? Did the disciples or someone else steal his body? It's not likely. Highly trained Roman soldiers guarded the tomb, and falling asleep on duty was punishable by death. Many have questioned if a Roman soldier could have removed the body. If one had, they would have paraded Jesus' body around the next day to prove Jesus had not risen.

Also his brothers, epistle authors James and Jude, became key leaders in the church after his resurrection. How could his brothers, who watched him grow up, believe that Jesus lived a sinless life unless he really did? I have two sons, and even though they are very close to one another, each would have no trouble coming up with a list of weaknesses or faults of his brother. The fact that James and Jude followed Jesus after his death speaks volumes.

Finally, his disciples, who scattered like frightened mice when Jesus was arrested and crucified, boldly returned to start the church after they saw their resurrected Savior with their own eyes and heard his Great Commission with their ears. All of the disciples except John (who was tortured) were martyred for their faith, including Peter, who asked for and received permission to be crucified upside down because he didn't feel worthy to be crucified in the same manner as Jesus. If the resurrection were just a hoax, why would they all suffer so much? None of them would have died for a lie.

If you want to explore more evidence pertaining to Christ's resurrection, consider reading William Lane Craig's book, *On Guard: Defending Your Faith with Reason and Precision.*[1] It's one of the best books I've read on defending your faith and growing in your understanding of Christian apologetics. I'd also encourage you to visit www.everystudent.com to find answers to your questions about the resurrection, the existence of God, the reliability of the Bible, and other questions you have.

When I was a freshman in college, I partied during a weekend trip with several fraternity brothers. I had too much to drink that Saturday night and woke up the next morning with a miserable hangover. I remember thinking to myself, *It's Easter Sunday, and this is the first time I haven't gone to church on Easter*. I then just brushed off the thought and went on to party some more with my fraternity brothers.

At that time, I wasn't convinced intellectually or spiritually that the resurrection took place. I had accepted my parents' view of the resurrection but hadn't explored the evidence myself. It is too easy to believe superficially about a traditionally accepted story.

I've found that beliefs like that tend to fall apart or fall away and offer little help in the face of temptation.

A lot of us are like that. We celebrate Easter out of tradition, but when we don't absolutely believe intellectually that it happened, it doesn't become part of our spiritual center. Not knowing the power of Jesus' resurrection and what it means to us, we are not affected much in our daily lives.

When we do believe it took place and understand the depth of its meaning, it becomes a central part of our spiritual psyche and takes on more meaning for us than it would if Jesus were just a myth or legend like the Easter Bunny.

Easter Sunday is a special day because it was the day the door opened for people to have a love relationship with God. It's a special day because we begin to understand the power of the resurrection, which transforms us into the very image of our Lord and Savior.

In short, when we believe that Christ really died on the cross for our sins and that he rose again from the dead, it's easier to be "All In" with God.

Being "All In"

A popular phrase in sports is "All In." I believe Dabo Swinney, the head football coach of the Clemson Tigers, was one of the first college coaches to use the phrase in regard to winning in football, but others quickly caught on. I recently noticed the Fellowship of Christian Athletes ministry has adopted "All In" as its tag line.

The phrase is pretty self-explanatory. To be "All In" means that you're focused. You've bought into the philosophy. You're sold. You've sacrificed other priorities that you've deemed less important so that you can be "All In" for what is very important to you.

In 1 Kings 6, Solomon constructed the Israelite temple, the very first building in which to worship God. However, some clues indicate that Solomon wasn't "All In" regarding his relationship with God.

First, seated right in the middle of the Bible's description of the building of the temple are twelve verses describing the building of Solomon's own house: "Solomon was building his own house thirteen years, and he finished his entire house" (1 Kgs. 7:1). Anyone who has ever built a home knows how much the planning, designing, and details occupy one's thoughts and attention. This was likely a great distraction to Solomon.

Also, while it only took him seven years to build the temple, it took him twice as long to complete his own house. He clearly was focusing his time and energy to make sure it was perfect.

Finally, each separate part of Solomon's house was nearly as large as the entire temple. The temple was built with *some* cedar, but the House of the Forest of Lebanon (a part of Solomon's housing complex used as an armory) was built with so much expensive cedar that it was named after the forest from which the cedar came. Solomon even made sure that the house of Pharaoh's daughter was nearly as large as the temple, while she practiced idolatry and didn't believe in God.

Because Solomon wasn't "All In," eventually the Pharaoh's daughter and Solomon's other foreign wives led him to walk away from God to worship idols and statues as they did. His divided heart resulted in Israel's becoming a divided kingdom.

Like Solomon, we're often guilty of not being "All In" when it comes to God. We constantly get distracted the way Solomon did when he was building God's temple. We give other people, our children, our work, or our hobbies first place in our lives instead of God, leading us to have a divided heart like Solomon's. But it doesn't have to be this way.

Jesus didn't come to earth to die on the cross so that he could be just a passenger in our lives. He really didn't. Christ died so that he can have first place in our lives. When we commit to being "All In," he pours out his love on us, empowers us with the Holy Spirit to be more than conquerors, and blesses us with the abundant life he promised in John 10:10.

What about you? Are you "All In" when it comes to God?

Being "All In" means you're doing the very best you can to follow God's Great Commandment: "You shall love the Lord your God with all your heart and with all your soul and with all your mind" (Matt. 22:37).

It's not always easy, just as being a good son to my mom and dad, husband to Elizabeth, and father to my kids isn't always easy. It's something I have to work on and be intentional with every day. I can move closer to my family one day if I am intentional, and then I can slowly grow more distant from them if I'm not.

It's the same with God. When we're intentional in pursuing him and love him in all three areas, our hearts, souls, and minds, we feel closer to him. If we go a few days or weeks without being intentional, we'll feel more distant.

Now's the time to give him first place in your life. Being "All In" may look different for each of us as we discover how we can best serve God with our time, talents, and abilities. The important thing is that we don't wait, that we move toward loving God more now before we miss out on what he has in store for us.

It's easier to do when you understand the value of Christ. Jesus is worth so much more than everything else in our lives put together, and if we give him the keys and allow him to have the driver's seat of our lives, he makes everything better. Commit to being "All In" with God, and experience the abundant life full of joy and love. I make you this promise: if you do, your life will be full of more adventure than you've ever imagined.

Note

[1]William Craig, *On Guard*, Kindle edition.

Author Note

After I'm done reading a book, I always like to look back and reflect on what I've learned. When I don't take notes while reading, then I sometimes forget what each chapter's about. The following are chapter summaries to freshen your memory as you look back, remember what you've read, and come up with a couple of action steps to take as you seek to develop your love for God.

Chapter One—Somebody's Watching Us
When we try to find our identity in something besides Christ, we suffer from an identity crisis. By taking the time to know God, we can find our identity in Christ, in whom we find our strength and security.

Chapter Two—Finding Real Joy
We all try to find joy in things other than Christ, such as what we do or what others think of us. Real joy can only be found in Christ, and we can never stray so far away from God that he won't run out to meet us when we return to him.

Chapter Three—The Pearl of Great Value
Christ is the pearl of great value. The only way we can walk away from counterfeit pearls in our lives is by understanding the value of knowing Christ.

Chapter Four—Attack of the Caterpillar
This chapter is related to the last one in that it shows how we can best understand the value of knowing Christ— by studying God's Word. We live in a fast-paced society, and it's easy to find ourselves

too busy to spend time with God. This chapter explores the dangers of not taking the time to know God, as well as the benefits of remembering the gospel daily.

Chapter Five—I Will Go Where You Want Me to Go

The first area of devotion to God involves going where he wants us to go. God has a great adventure planned for us, but sometimes our fear gets in the way and keeps us from experiencing all God has for us. If we surrender ourselves by going where he wants, we can experience a life better than we imagined.

Chapter Six—I Will Do What You Want Me to Do

Once we ask Christ into our lives, we become new creations. By the power of the Holy Spirit, we can now live holy lives, pleasing to the Lord. This chapter battles some of the misconceptions people have about being holy. First of all, real joy is found when we live holy lives. Secondly, holiness is possible, even in the area of sexual purity. Finally, our holiness should also be reflected in the way we think.

Chapter Seven—I Will Say What You Want Me to Say

We've all developed bad habits of saying what we want to say whenever we want to say it. When we surrender our words to Jesus, lives around us are changed.

Chapter Eight—I Will Give What You Want Me to Give

When we gave our lives to God, we gave him everything, including our treasures. When we give our finances over to the Lord, our heart goes toward him and his purposes.

Chapter Nine—Beware of Green Biscuits!

Even in Jesus' day, his message of salvation was hard to believe (John 6:66), and it hasn't gotten any easier to believe today. This chapter addresses the belief that there can't be just one true religion.

Chapter Ten—When Darkness Fell

Many believers as well as skeptics struggle with why a good God would allow evil and suffering. This chapter helps the reader to reconcile this struggle.

Chapter Eleven—Shooting Fireworks at Cars Is a Bad Idea

The sacredness of choice is one of the ideals embraced by today's culture, and it's one of the reasons young people struggle with the Bible and Christianity. This chapter helps the reader to see that freedom is not such a simple thing and that boundaries can actually lead to freedom.

Chapter Twelve—A Death-Defying Stunt on Thrill Hill

Many who don't believe in Christ have been pushed away because of Christian hypocrisy and because of some Christians' bad driving records. This chapter helps the reader understand why Christians can't be expected to have a perfect record and also points out the great record the church has.

Chapter Thirteen—It All Comes Down to Easter Sunday

Ultimately the resurrection of Jesus of Nazareth is the cornerstone of Christian faith. If Jesus was not raised from the dead, then the Christian faith is a sham. If he was resurrected, then Jesus of Nazareth was God as he claimed to be. We must weigh the evidence behind the resurrection of Jesus and decide for ourselves if he is who he said he was.

About the Author

Chad Young works in full-time college ministry, serving as Cru Global's national director over the southeast region, leading the ministries in Florida, Georgia, Alabama, and Mississippi. He has served on the staff of Cru for fourteen years. He is the author of *Authenticity: Real Faith in a Phony, Superficial World* (InterVarsity Press), a discipleship-training manual, and magazine articles for *Worldwide Challenge* and *The Collegiate*. He frequently speaks at retreats and conferences and regularly writes devotionals for his website, FindingAuthenticChristianity.com. Chad, with his wife, Elizabeth, travels the country to speak at churches and teach church leaders how to make biblical disciples.

Chad currently resides in Atlanta, Georgia, with his wife, Elizabeth, and their four children, Wyatt, Clark, Evelyn, and Josilynn. His hobbies include cheering on his kids in sports, following college football, and laughing with family around the backyard fire pit.

If you enjoyed this book, you'll love **Chad Young's**
Authenticity: Real Faith in a Phony, Superficial World,

available at Amazon.com and other online bookstores.

"All you Christians are just a bunch of hypocrites!"
Unfortunately comments like this, and the deep,
passionate emotion behind them, define today's
postmodern culture. Truth is, according to a
recent study by the Barna group, the number
one reason people reject Christianity is a lack
of authentic Christians among their peers.
Meanwhile, we are so busy "being" Christians
and "doing" Christian activities in our churches
that we aren't relating to people in a meaningful,
authentic way.

In *Authenticity*, Chad writes as a person who has struggled with a worldly lifestyle and the distractions of living in a busy culture. Through its anecdotes and relational tone, this book will lead believers on their journey toward authentic Christian faith.

Are you looking for free devotionals? Are you in need of direction on how to mentor someone? Visit Chad's website, www.findingauthenticchristianity.com to find free devotionals for a majority of the books of the Bible as well as resources you can use as you help someone else grow in their faith.